MODERN GEOMETRIC DESIGN

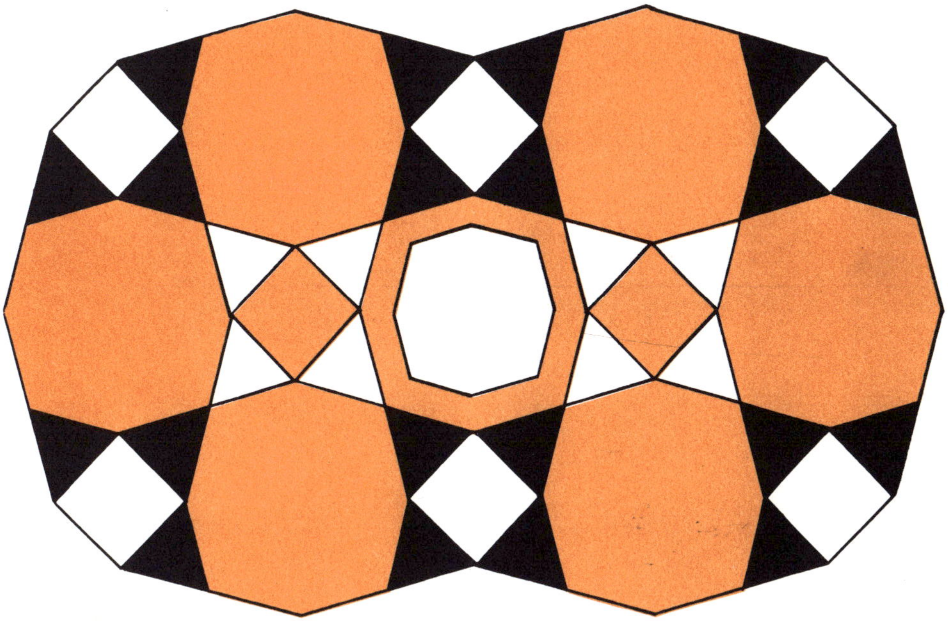

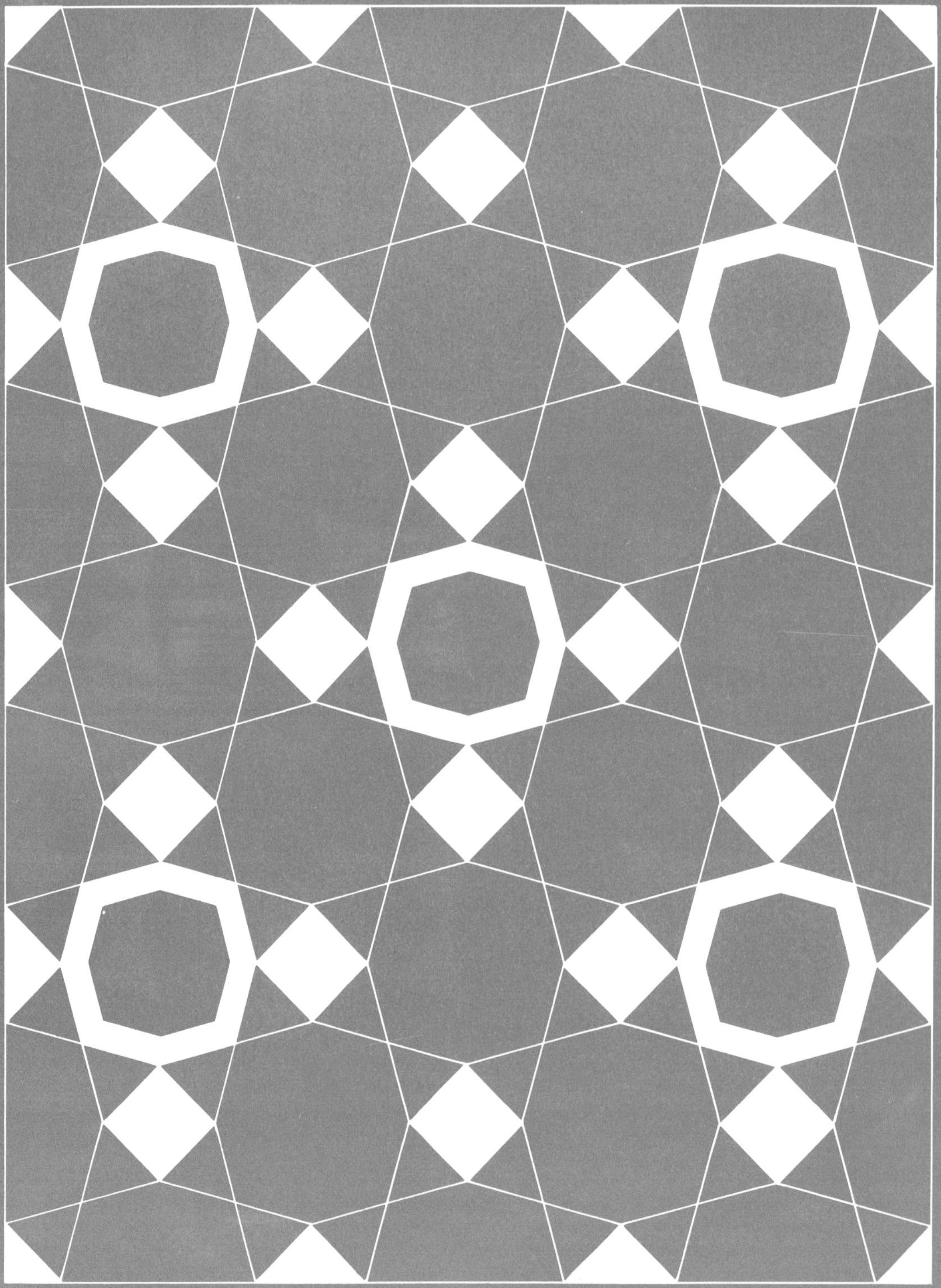

MODERN GEOMETRIC DESIGN

by Adolf Lorch

STERLING PUBLISHING CO., INC. NEW YORK

Oak Tree Press Co., Ltd.
Distributed by WARD LOCK, Ltd., London & Sydney

OTHER BOOKS OF INTEREST

Abstract Art
Acrylic and Other Water-Base Paints
Composition in Art
Designs—and How to Use Them
Experiments in Modern Art
Express Yourself in Drawing
Joy of Drawing
Painting Abstract Landscapes
Prints—from Linoblocks and Woodcuts
Techniques of Drawing

419 Park Avenue South, New York, N.Y. 10016
British edition published by Oak Tree Press Co., Ltd.
Distributed in Great Britain and the Commonwealth by
Ward Lock, Ltd., 116 Baker Street, London W1
The original edition was published in Germany

Manufactured in the United States of America

Library of Congress Catalog Card No.: 72-151714
ISBN 0-8069-5164-8 UK 7061 2288 7
5165-6

> "Decorations are a matter of taste, but design, inherently pure and simple, is like a signal, a synthesis, the result of order. Creating designs requires a positive, unconditional discipline."
>
> ***Le Corbusier***

The creation of geometric designs need not be regarded as a mystifying experience; it is based on the simple relationships of arcs, angles, and straight lines, which form circles, squares, triangles, rectangles and other geometric shapes. These, when assembled in a particular arrangement, can create a pleasing motif that may suggest plants, animals, masks, grimaces, or pure abstract patterns. Any one of the designs depicted in this book can be broken down into the basic geometric shapes. Your task is to arrange the shapes into an interesting design which you can then repeat or vary to create an attractive decoration.

Try a simple experiment. Take a black circle, a triangle and a rectangle and arrange them within a white square. When you are satisfied with the motif, draw another square next to it and repeat your design. Make a whole row of them. Then make another row of squares underneath the first row, this time using white shapes against a black background. Try alternating the white and black squares in checkerboard fashion. Put a black square after every two white squares. Try turning every other square upside down. Add more rows of squares. Make the squares the same color vertically, but alternate them horizontally. Make only the top half of the squares white and bottom half black. Reverse the colors of the shapes—circle, triangle, rectangle—accordingly. Change the size of the inner shapes or the size of the square.

You may prefer to draw a strictly symmetrical design, or you may wish to stress a particular pattern with your squares. The shapes within the squares can also join together to form a linkage. By now it should be quite evident that there is no end to the possibilities of geometric decorations or their applications.

The pattern you have created in this little experiment is known as an "unlimited surface decoration." As you have probably realized, this type of decoration can extend in any direction you wish. Such a technique is especially suitable for decorating wallpaper, rugs, drapes, ties and other textiles used in the house.

Another type of geometric design is the "limited decoration." This is intended for just one predetermined area and usually consists of one dominant motif. You can, however, reverse it consecutively from positive to negative, join it to rhythmic patterns which lead into another motif, or form a kaleidoscopic circle or any other polygonal shape.

Finally, there is the decoration tape or ribbon, which is mostly used for end seams of carpets, drapes and other textiles. It can be comprised of a limitless strip of motifs echoing or complementing the main surface area patterns. This is essentially a border decoration, but it can also provide an interesting break in your unlimited design, giving the viewer's eyes a chance to rest from the confusion of the over-all pattern.

The more proficient you become at creating geometric designs, the more sensitive you become to the mood implications. Certain combinations of circular shapes, for example, may produce a delicate easy-flowing design; hard triangular arrangements add excitement to the decoration.

The first nine pages of this collection offer hints and suggestions for the formulative construction of geometric designs. These examples are meant to indicate how the outline rests on basic forms, how the center-leg insert of a pair of compasses can enhance the designs, and how, by the mingling of various areas in a given motif and by careful selection of lights and darks, different decorative patterns can be elicited. The adjacent figures serve to show the consecutive order in which each project is to be prepared and finished. All the draft-outlines in this collection were created by these means.

The designs in the rest of the book are initially rendered in black and white to show their geometric abstraction and their positive-negative relationships. The juxtaposition of another color (in this case, orange) with black or white, however, results in a much softer contrast and can greatly affect the "mood" of your design. Combinations of orange, black and white can alter or lend interest to the original motif. With this in mind, we have attempted to show each rendition in first black and white, black or white with orange, and a combination of the three colors. This is intended to aid the artist in realizing the potentialities of the particular decoration.

The addition of a color to a black and white design opens up an unlimited range of possibilities. The color may be utilized in your designs as part of a repetitive unlimited pattern, or you can use it selectively and control it to bring another dimension into the design. For instance, you may choose to add color to only part of your decoration and thus create a single motif within the existing unlimited one, transforming the latter into a textural background. The occasional monotony of a repeated black and white pattern may be relieved considerably with a row or two of the same design in orange alone. The color can also be used to emphasize particularly interesting parts of your decoration (such as the plant and animal shapes your imagination sees in it) by accentuating only those areas. In many cases the use of color uncomplicates an especially complex design by directing your eye to certain areas first and consequently providing central points of interest. It may also serve as a backdrop in which black and white areas are stressed.

Once you have become thoroughly acquainted with the construction of the geometric designs and can copy or adapt the ones illustrated on these pages, experiment with the use of color. Recreate the designs using orange and black or white, and combinations of the three. After that, you will soon be able to draft and color your own newly improvised decorative patterns.

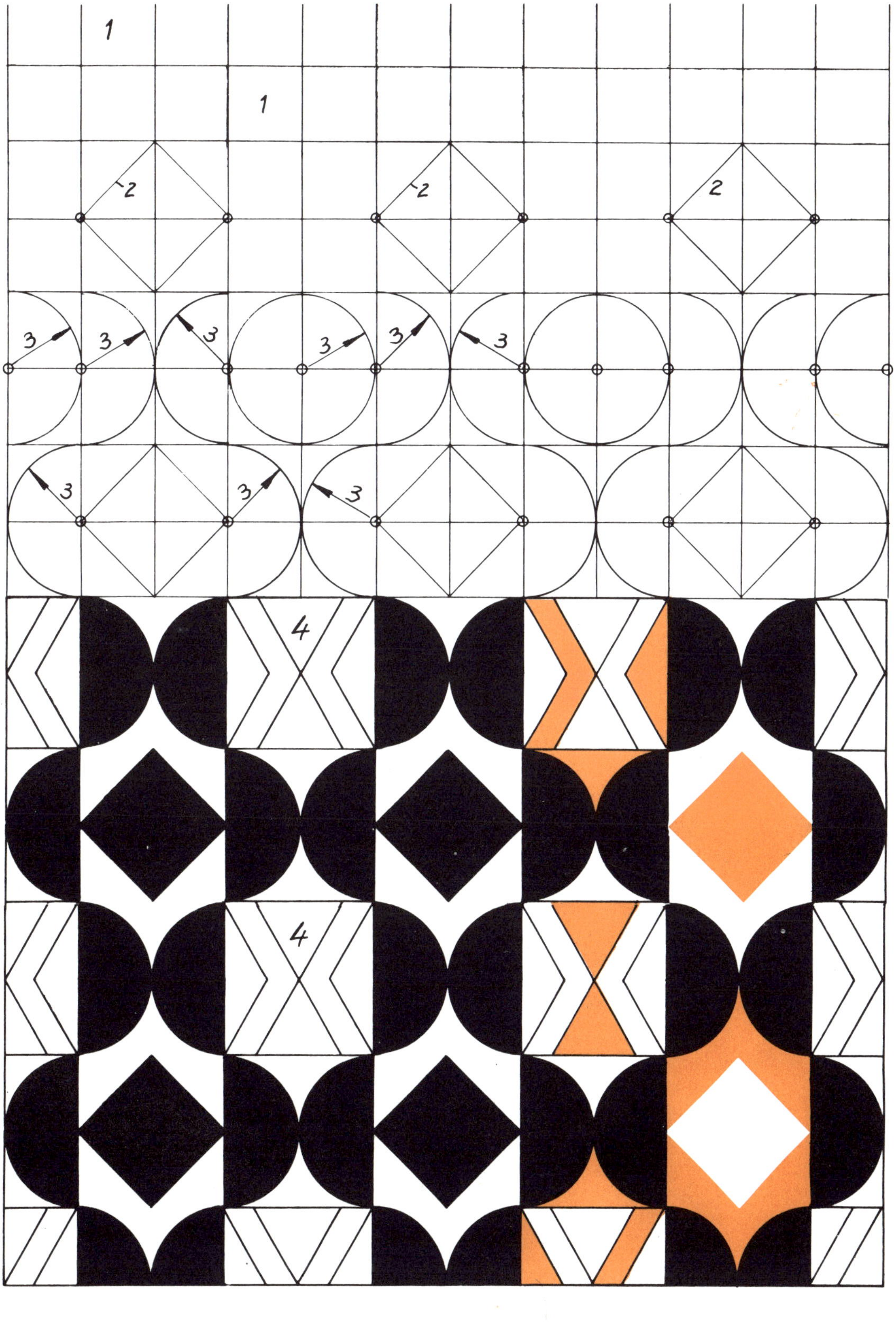
1
1
2
2
2
3
3
3
3
3
3
3
3
3
3
4
4

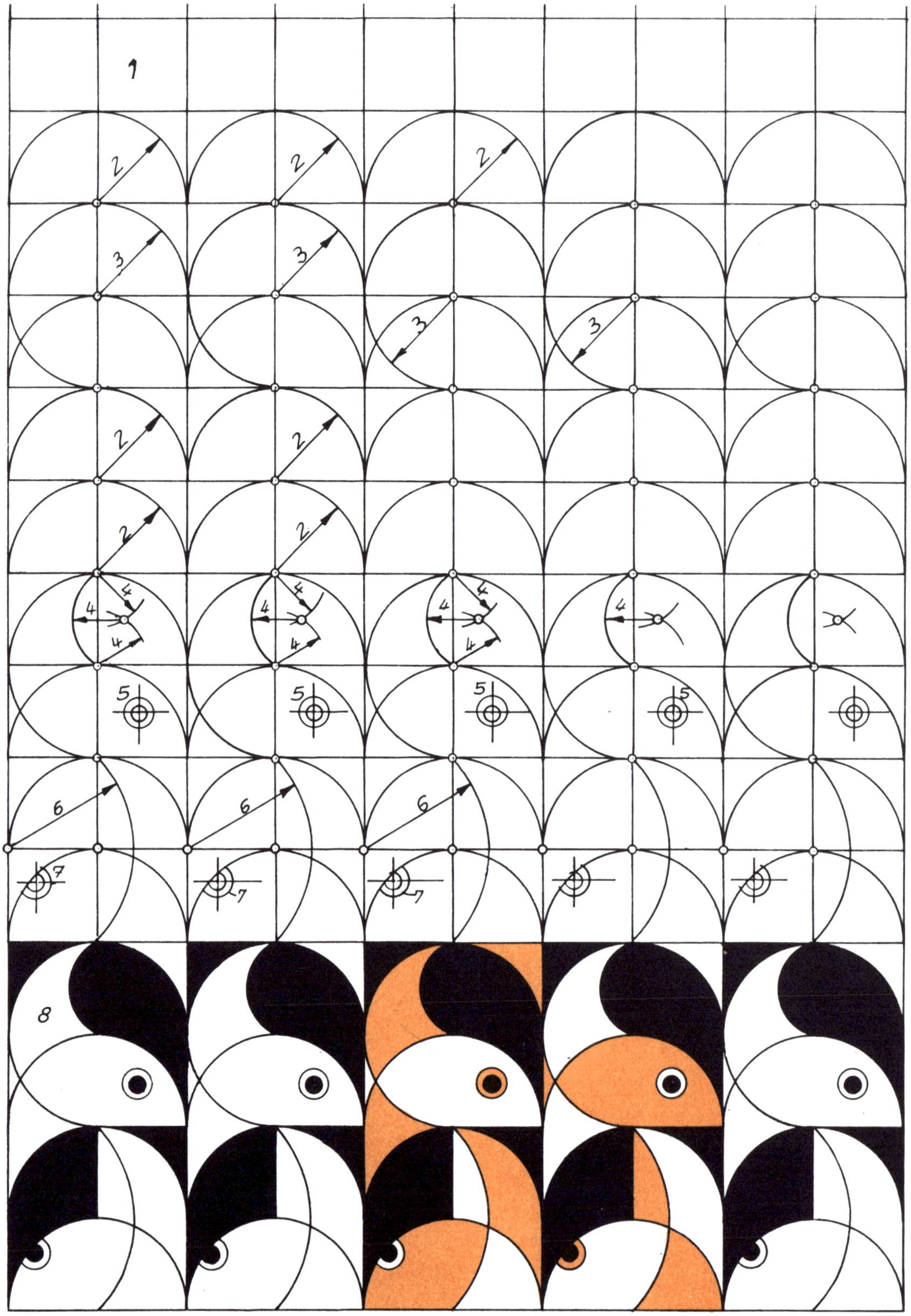
1
2
3
4
5
6
7
8

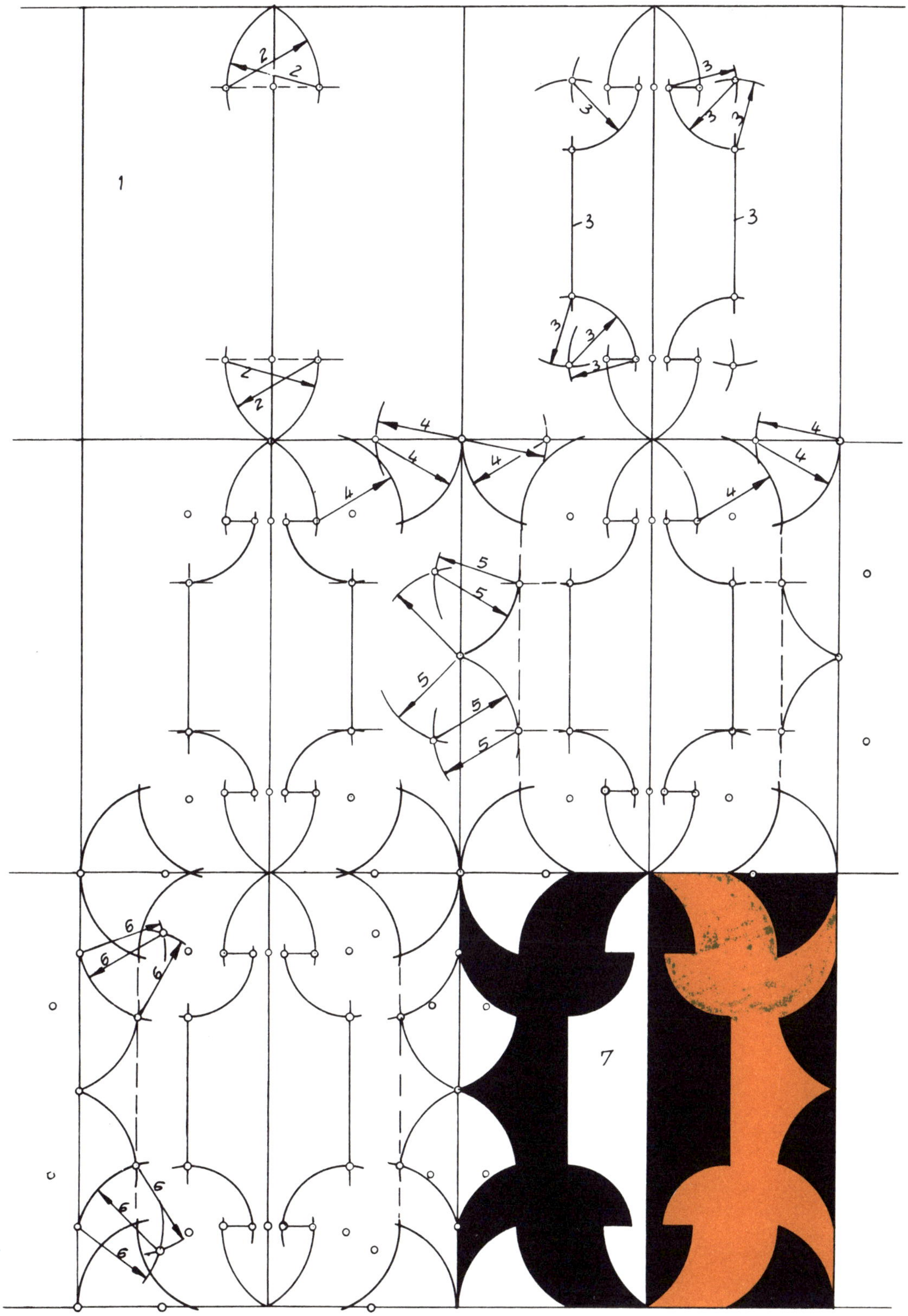
1
2
3
4
5
6
7

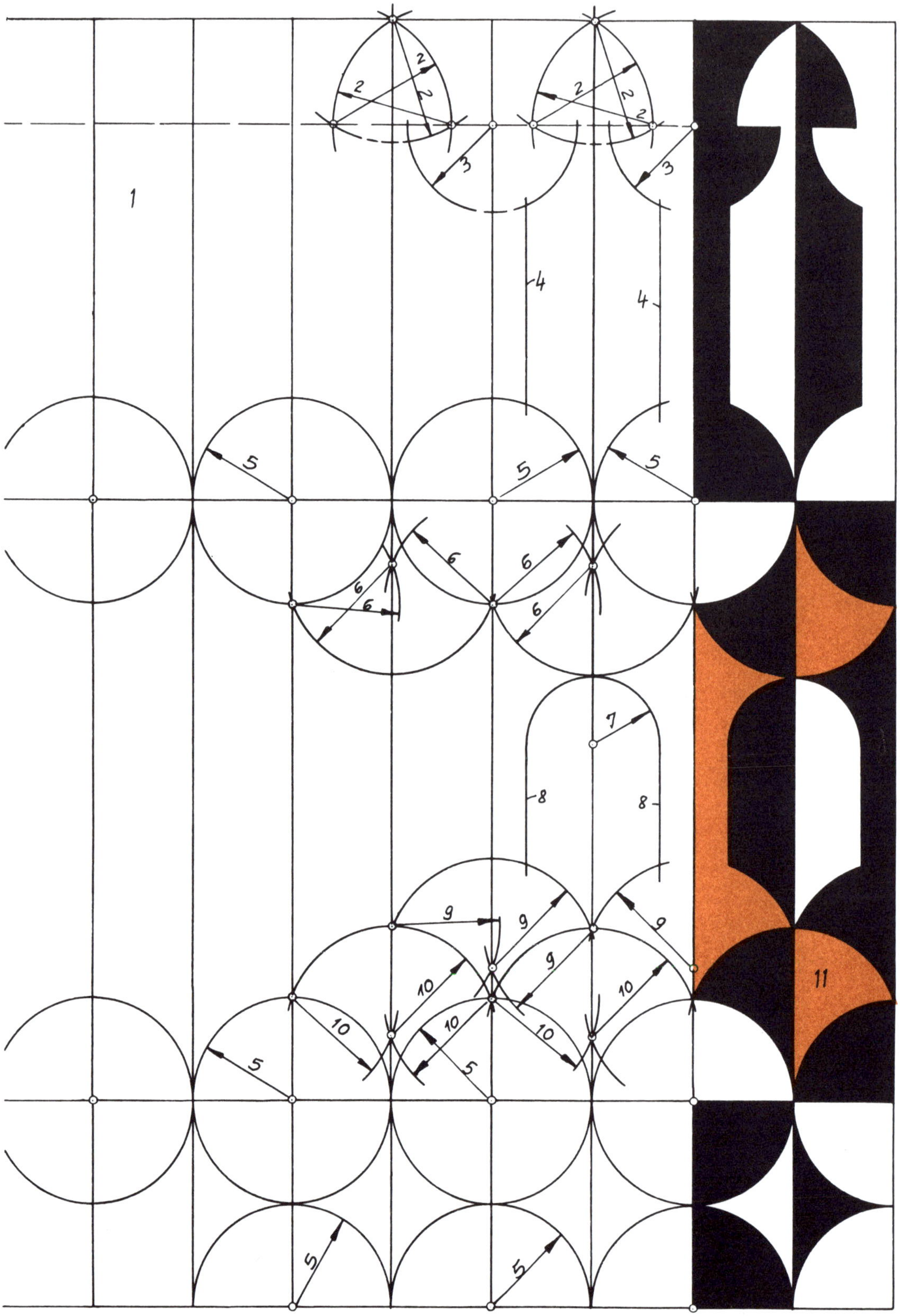
1
2
2
2
2
2
2
3
3
4
4
5
5
5
6
6
6
6
6
7
8
8
9
9
9
9
10
10
10
10
10
11
5
5
5
5

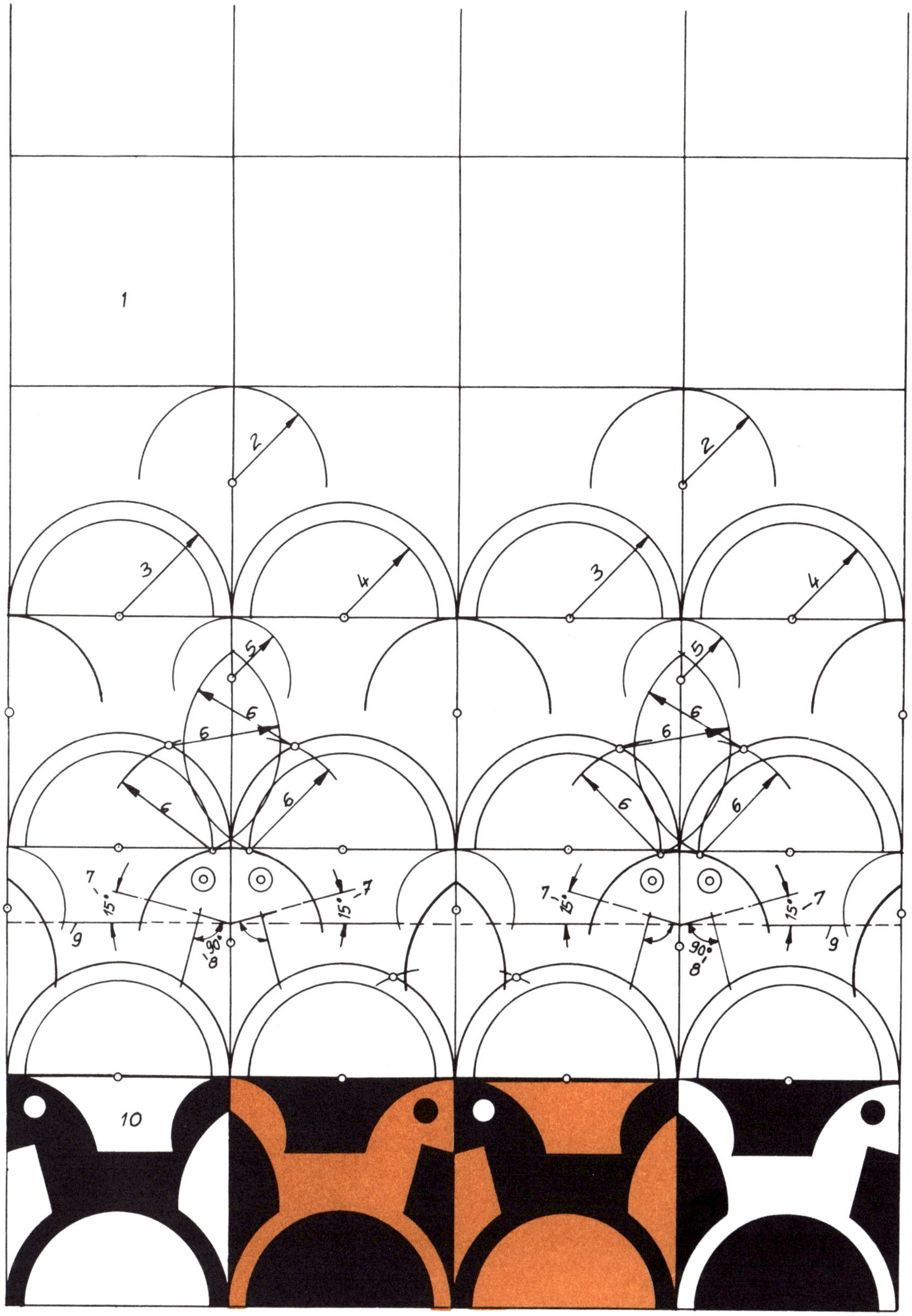
1
2
2
3
4
3
4
5
5
6
6
6
6
6
6
6
6
7
7
7
7
15°
15°
15°
15°
90°
90°
8
8
9
9
10

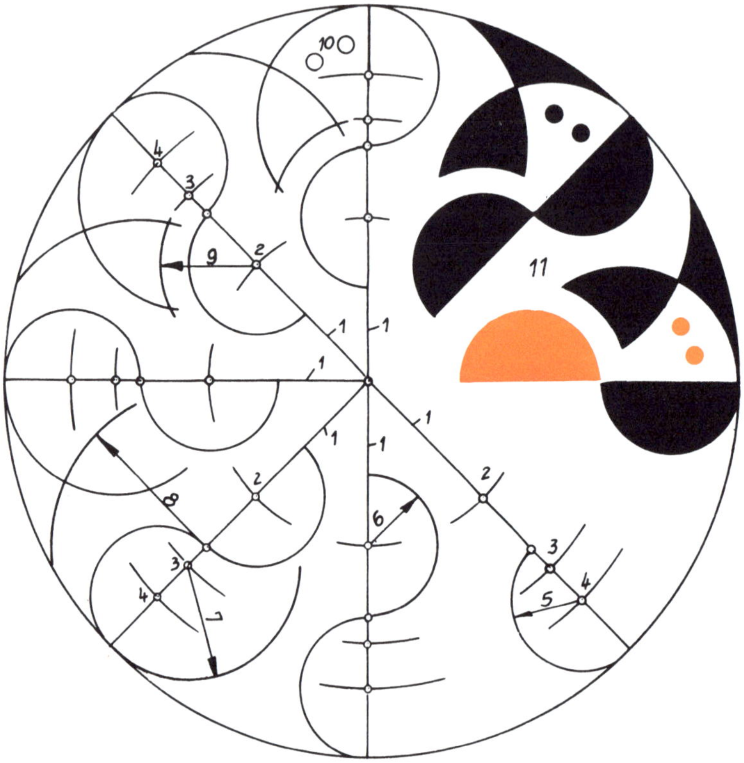

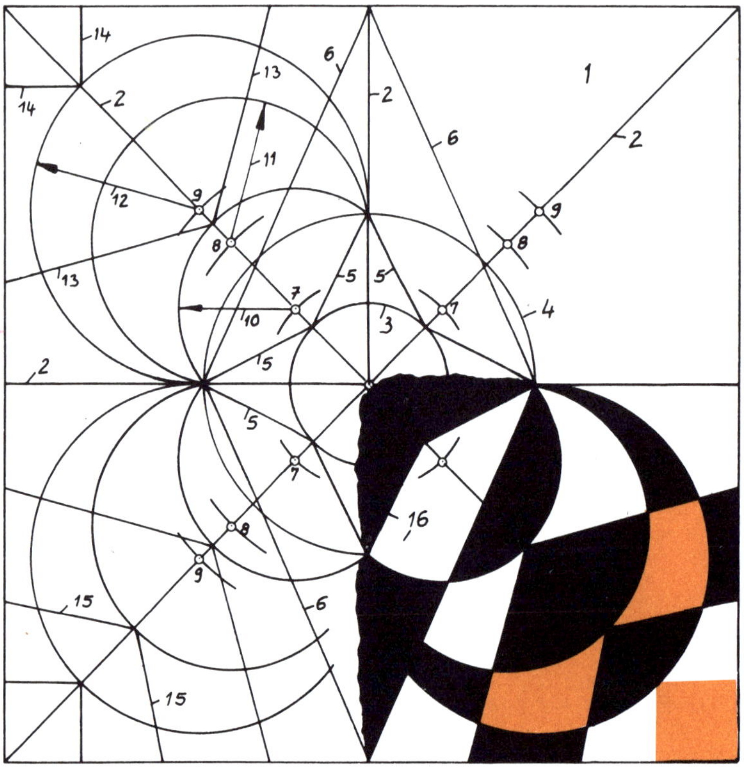

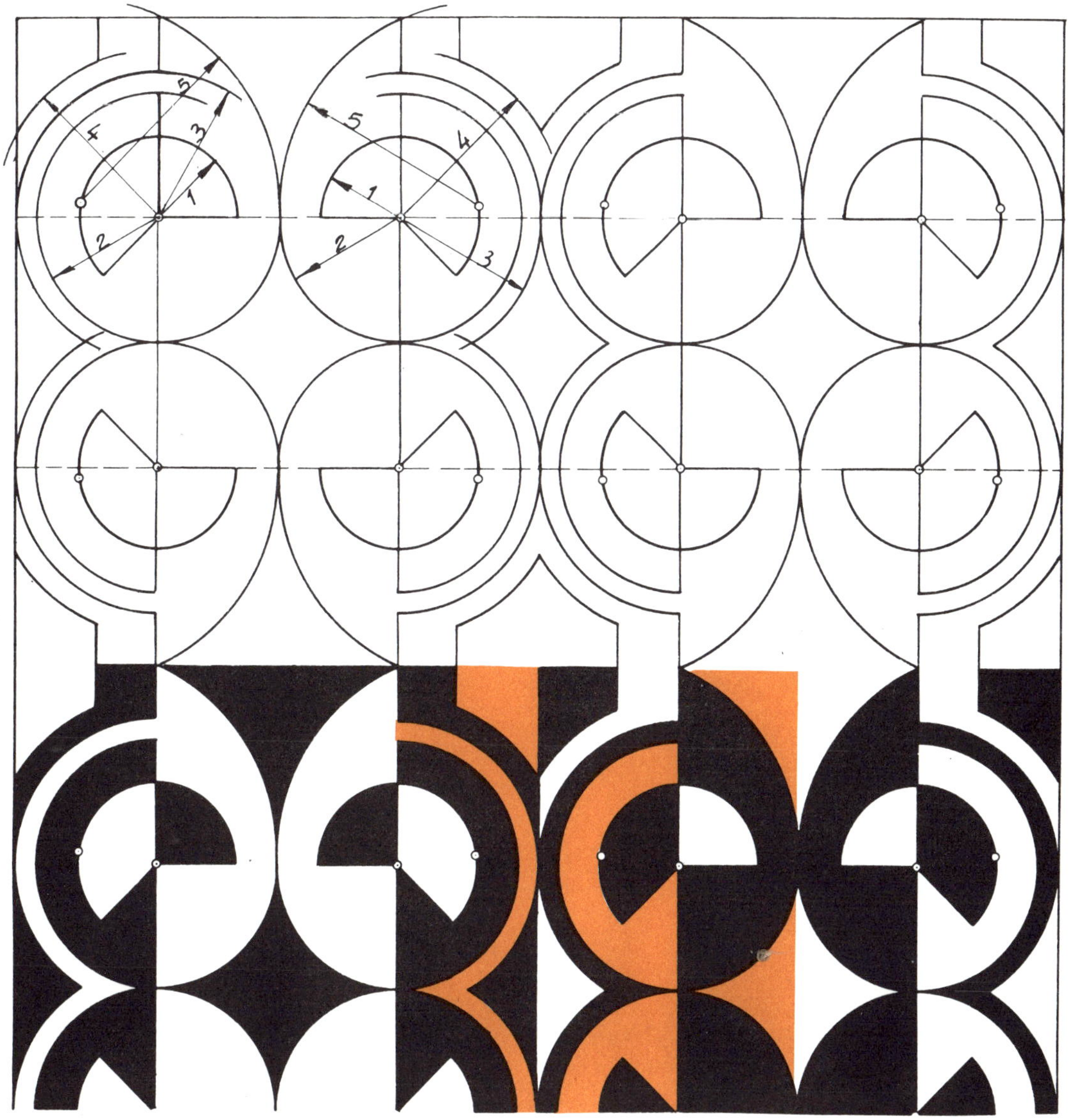

1
2
3
4
5

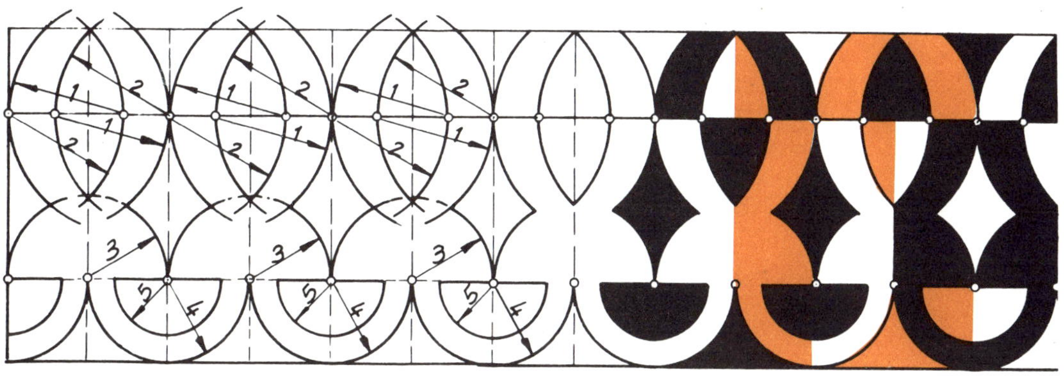

1
2
3
4
5

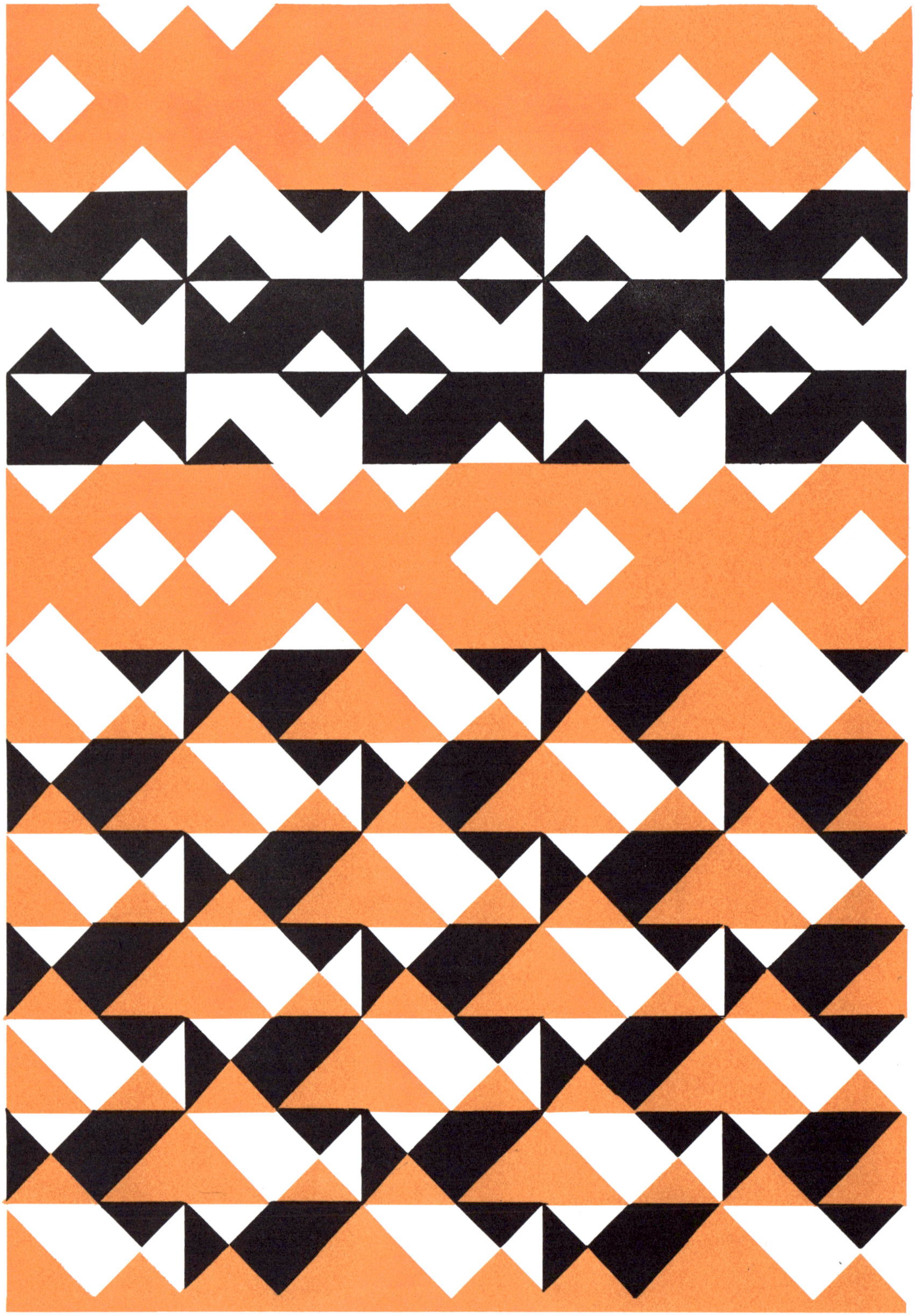

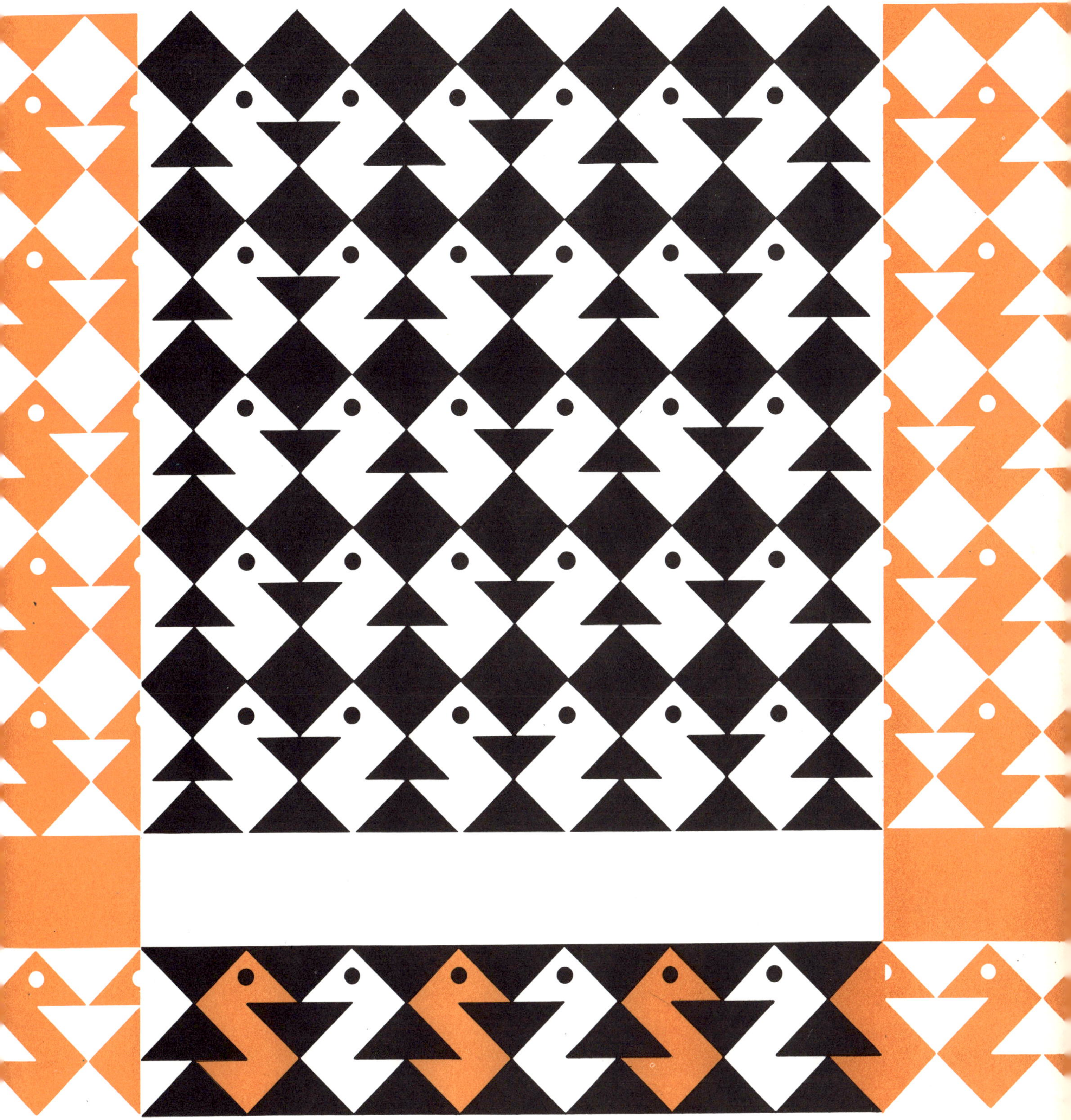

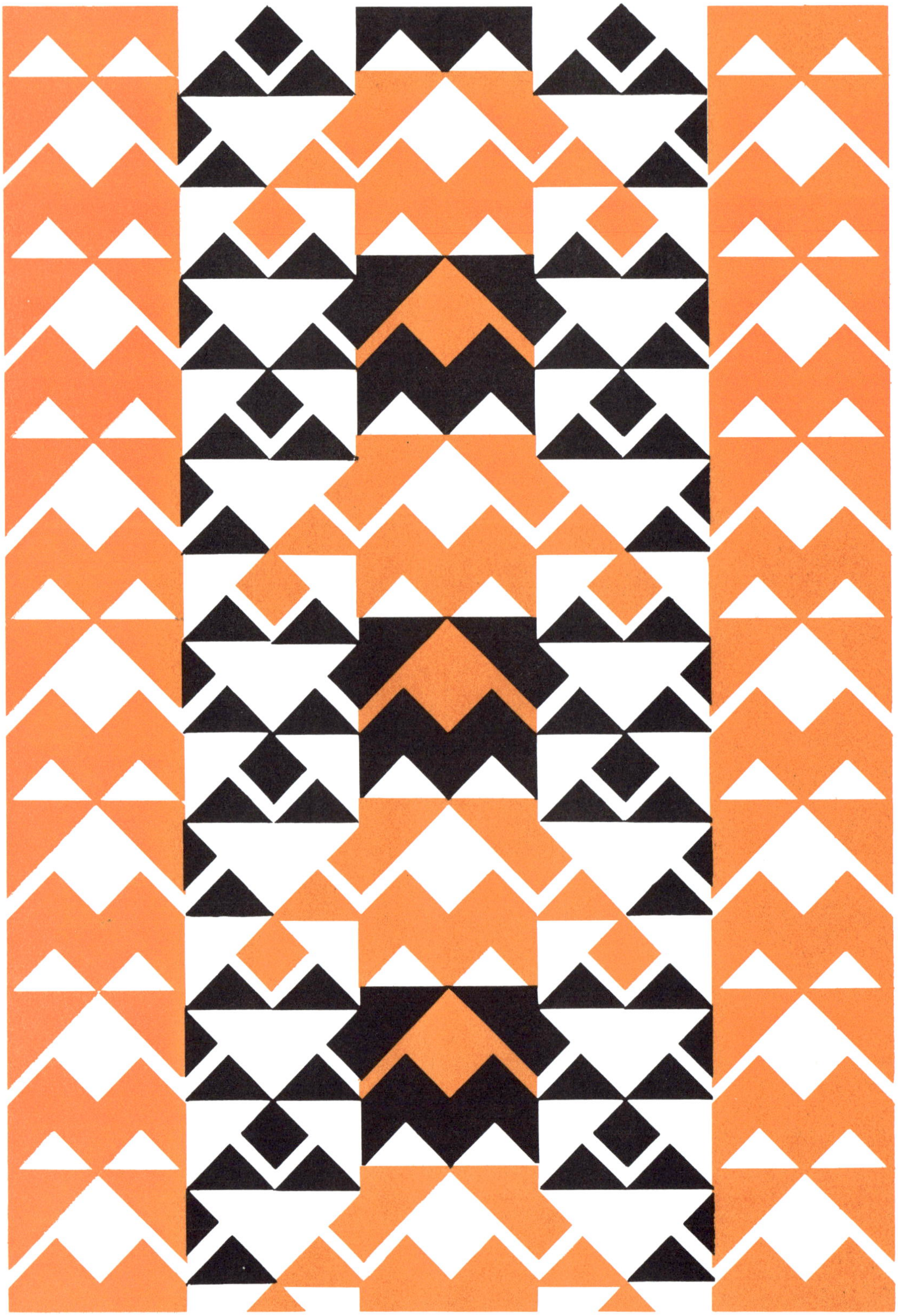

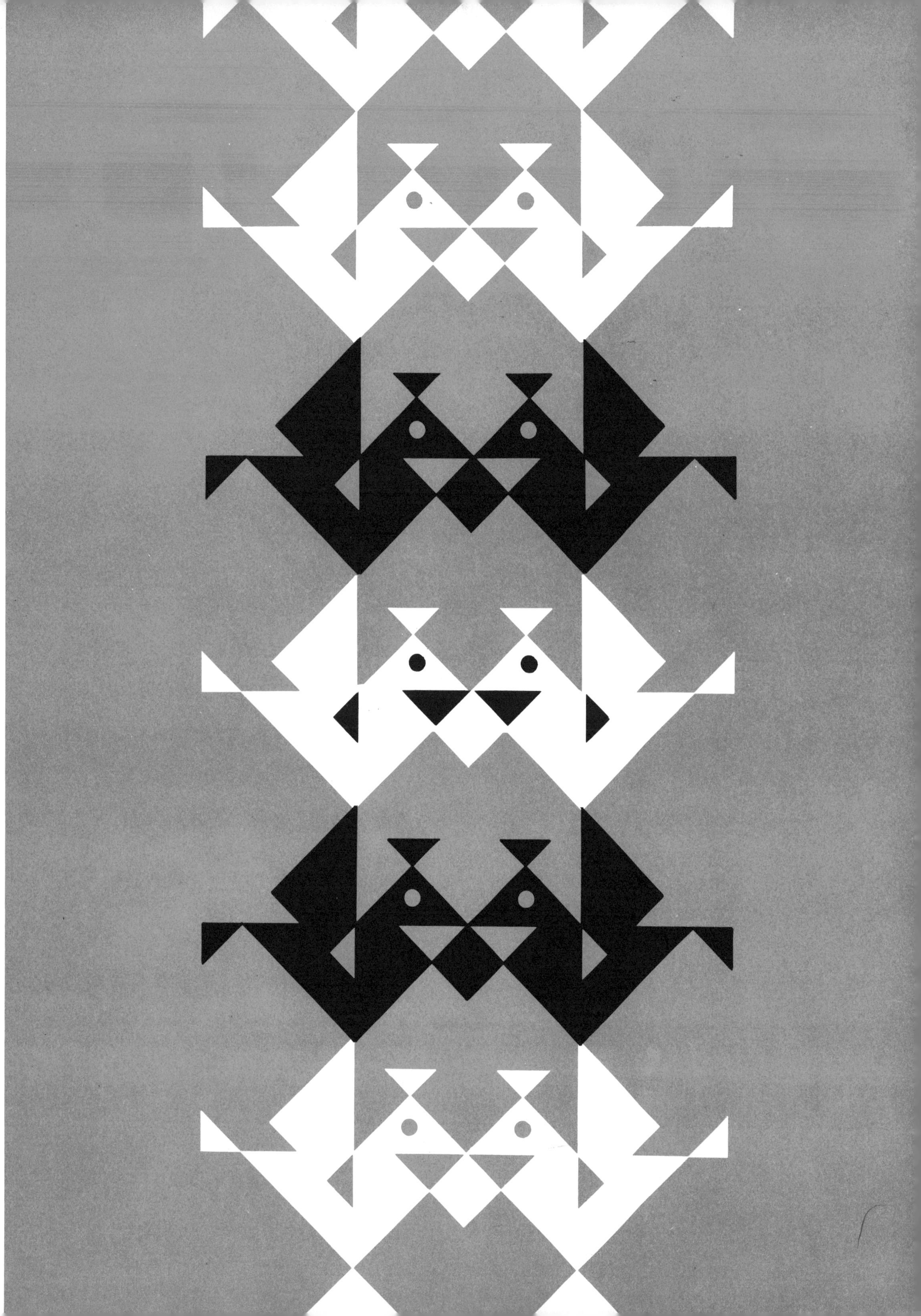

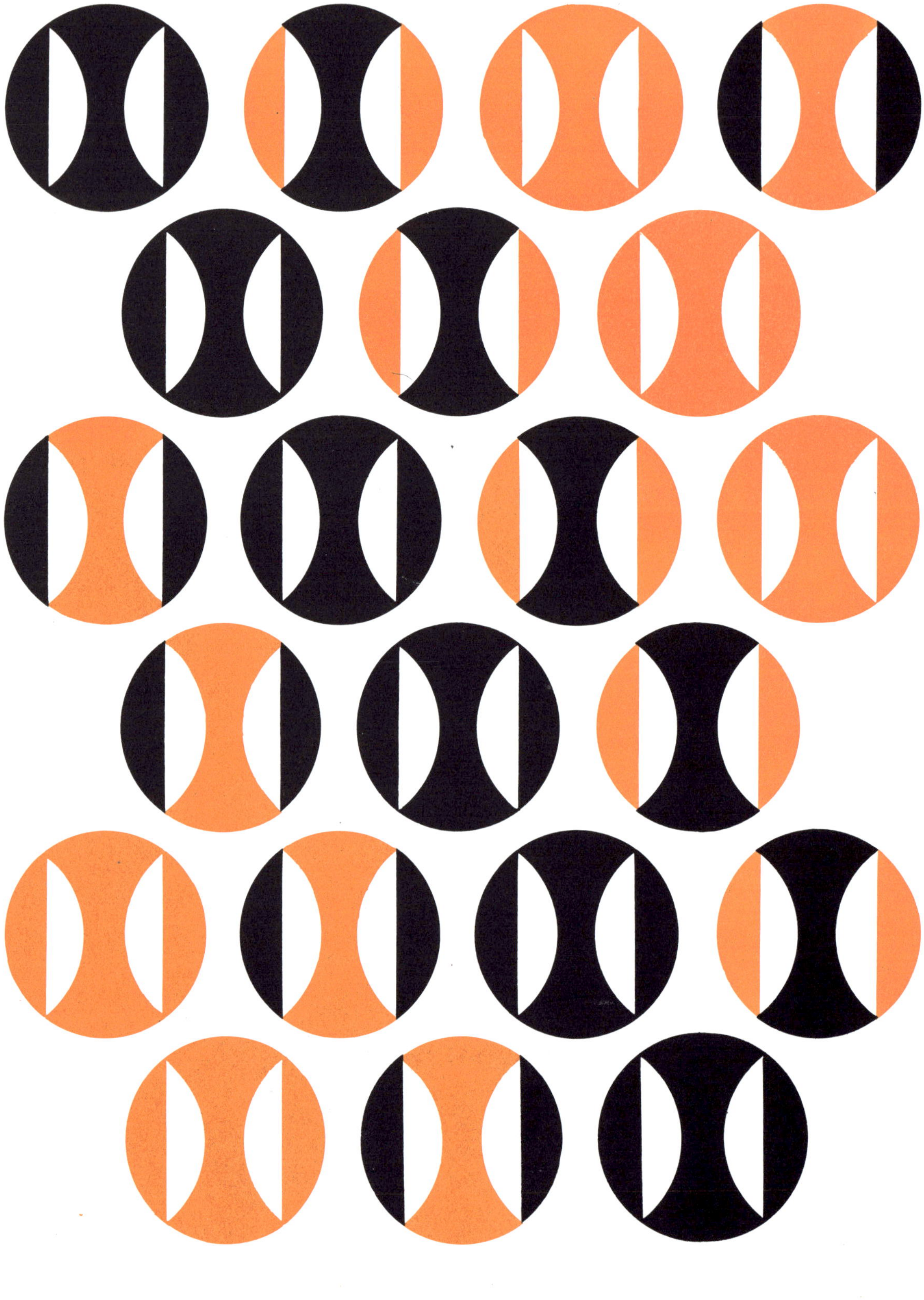

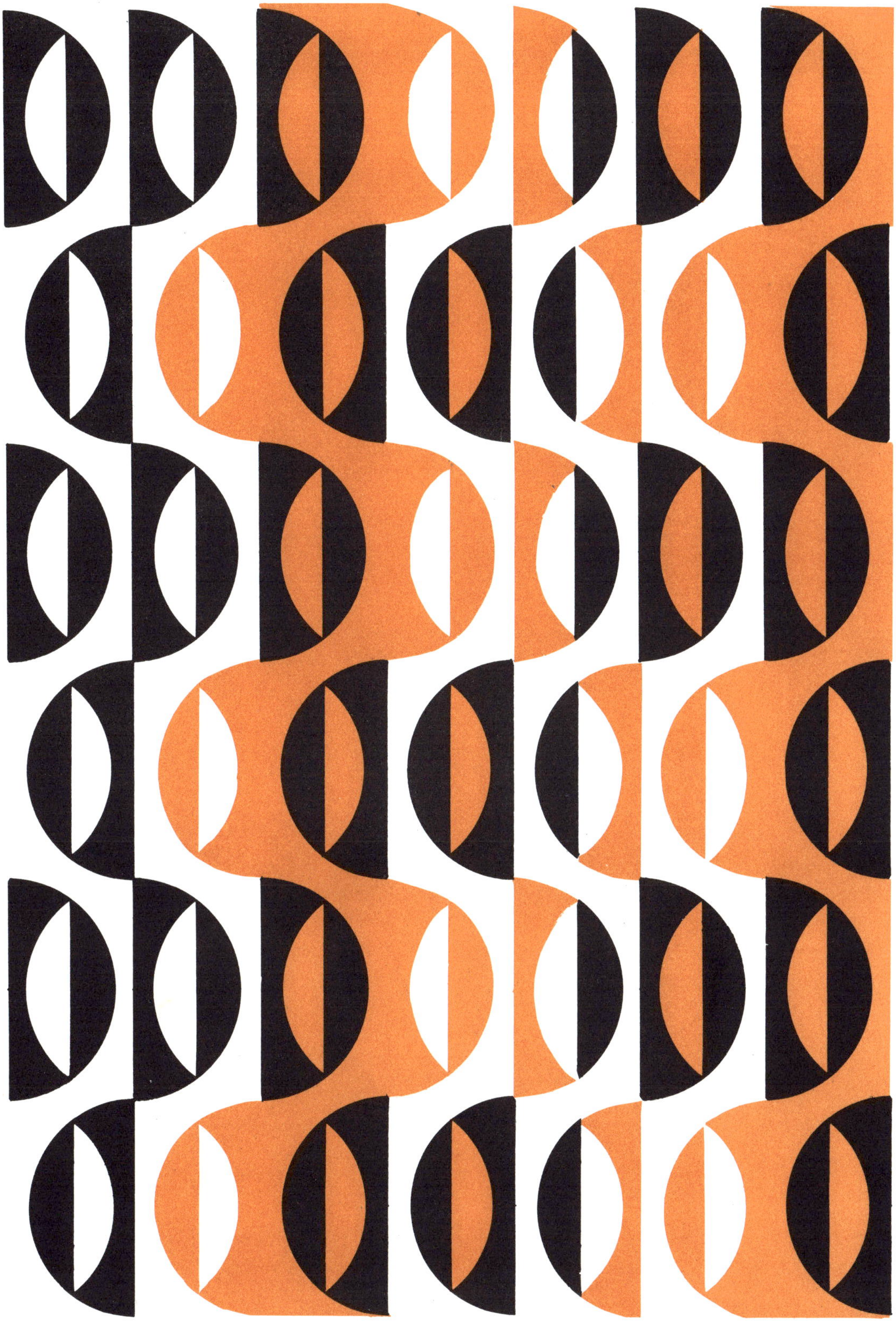

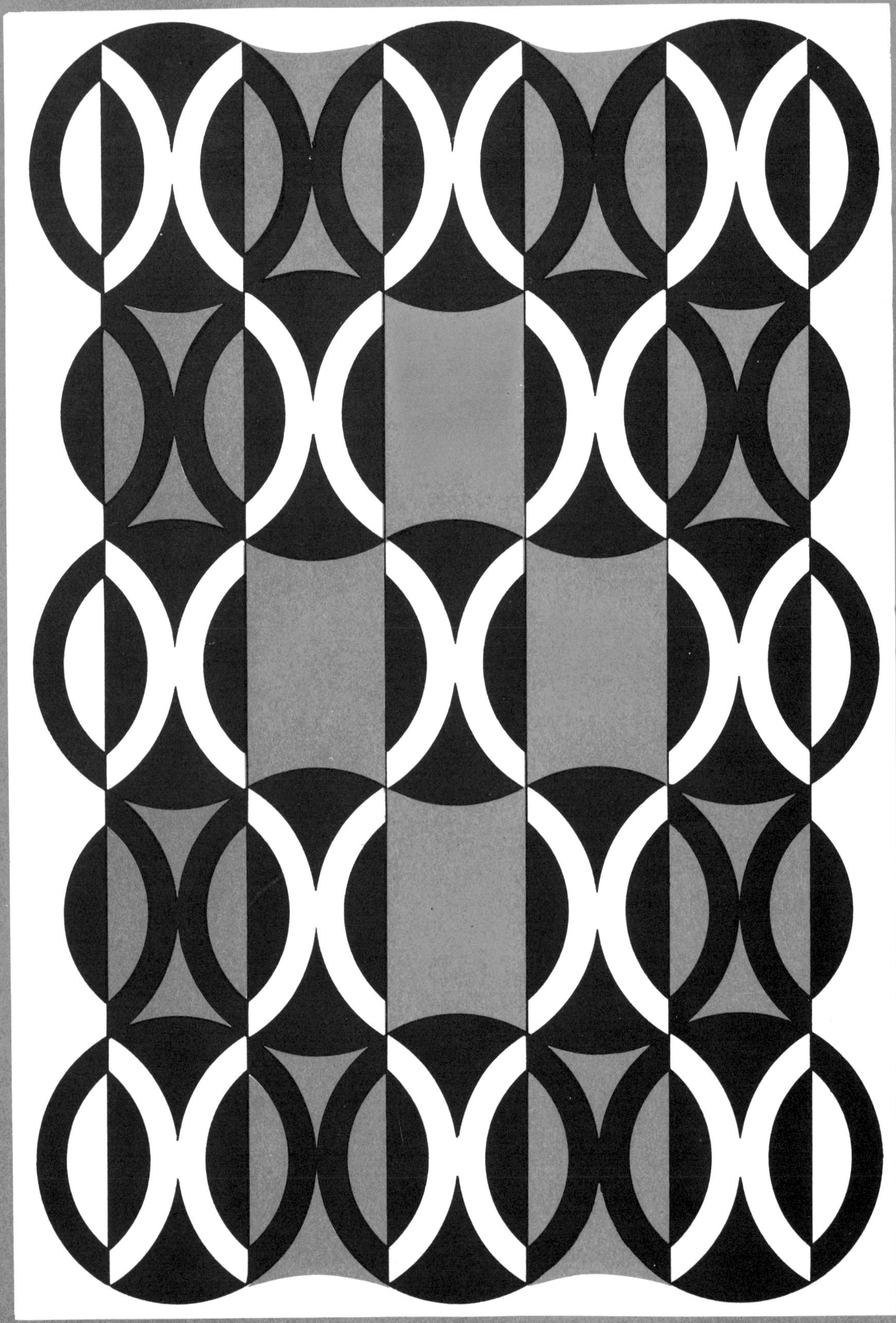

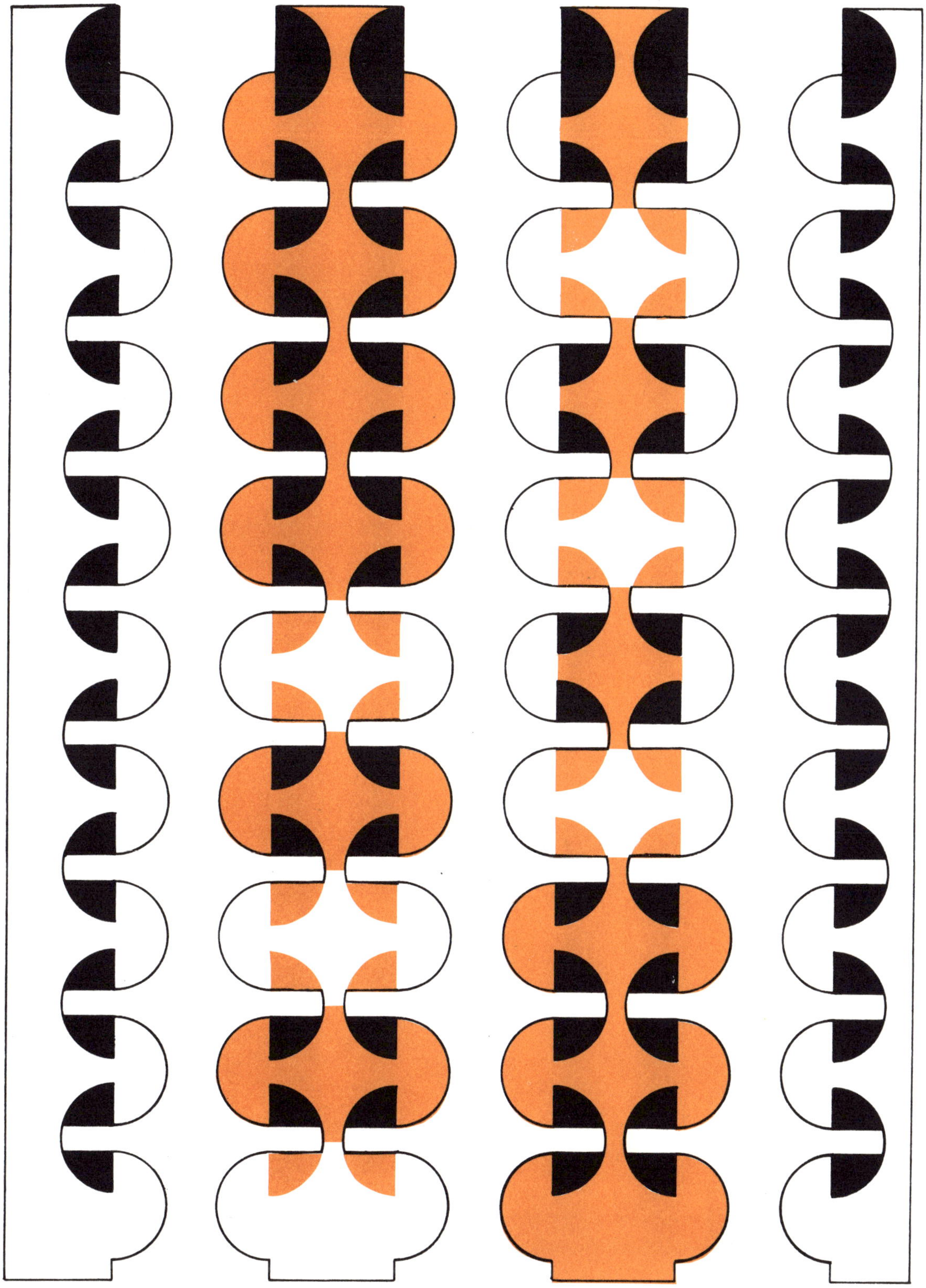

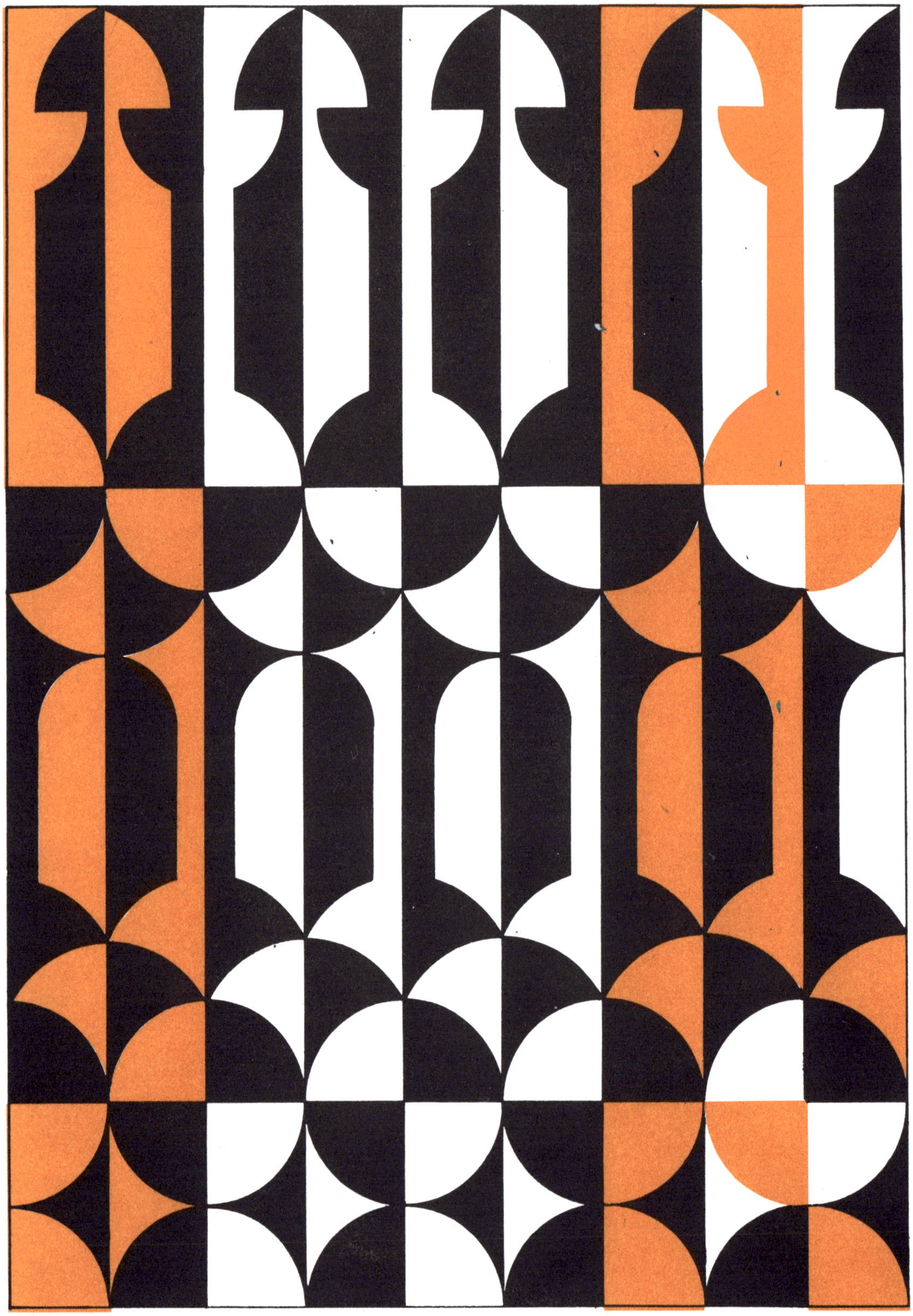

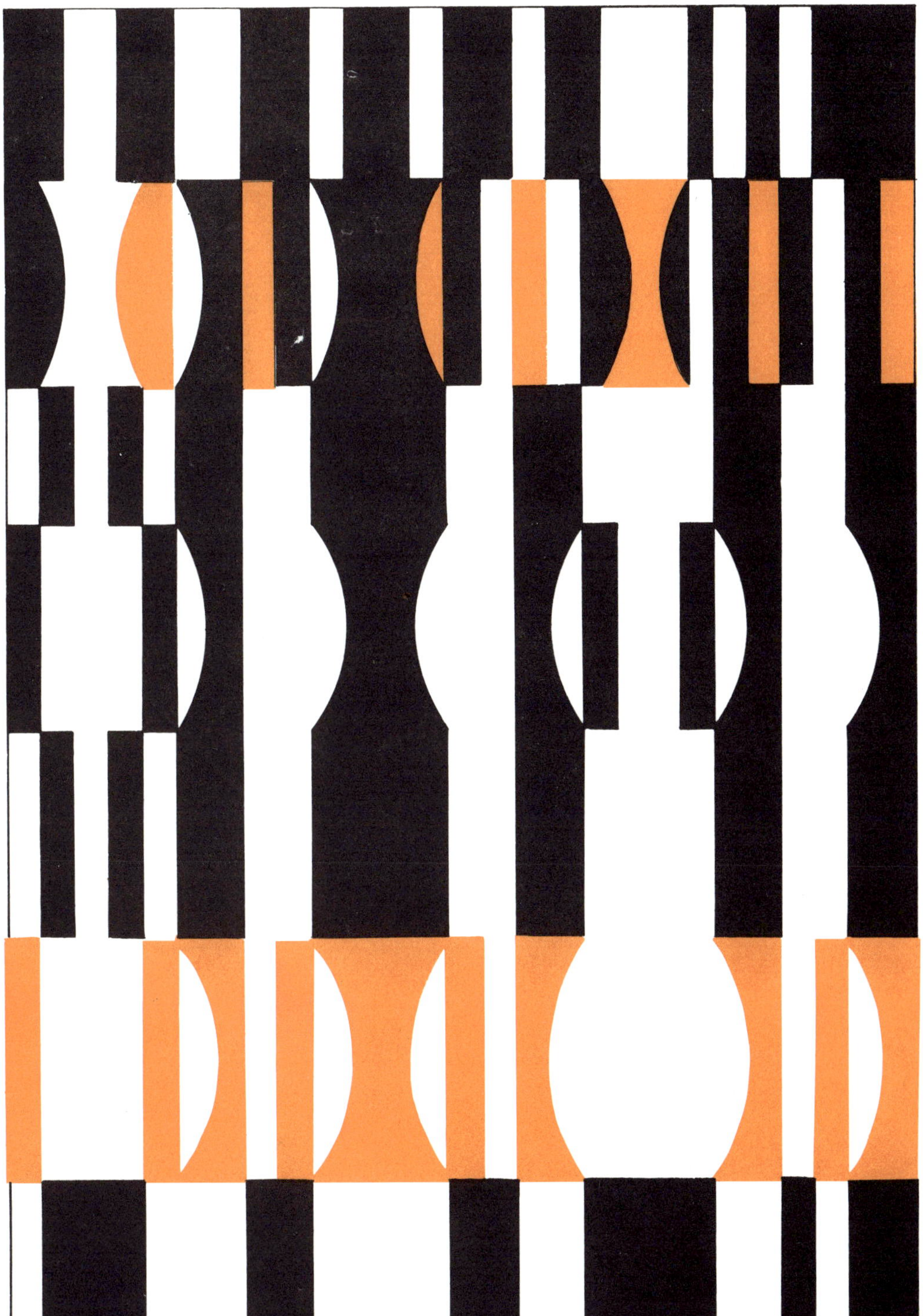

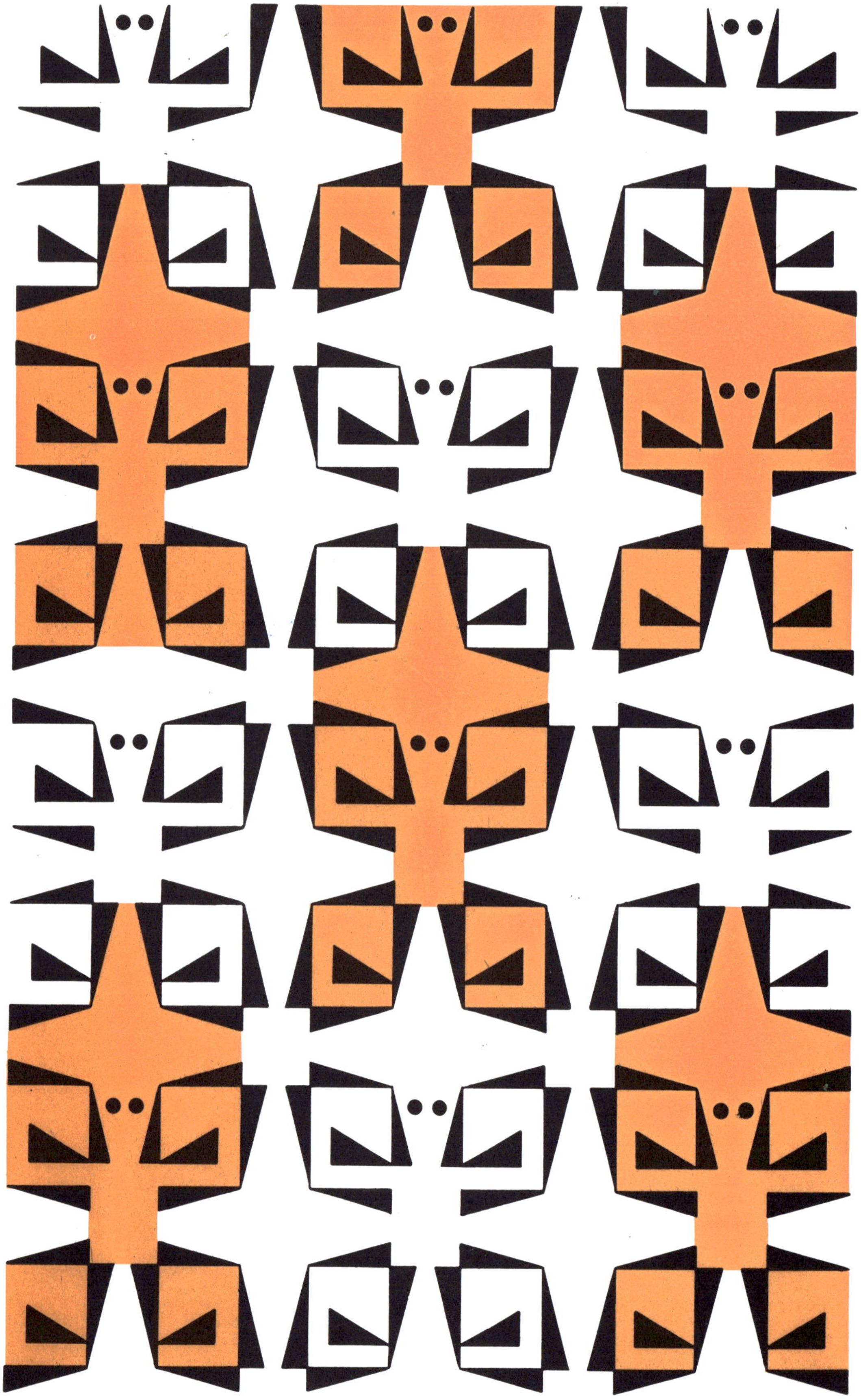

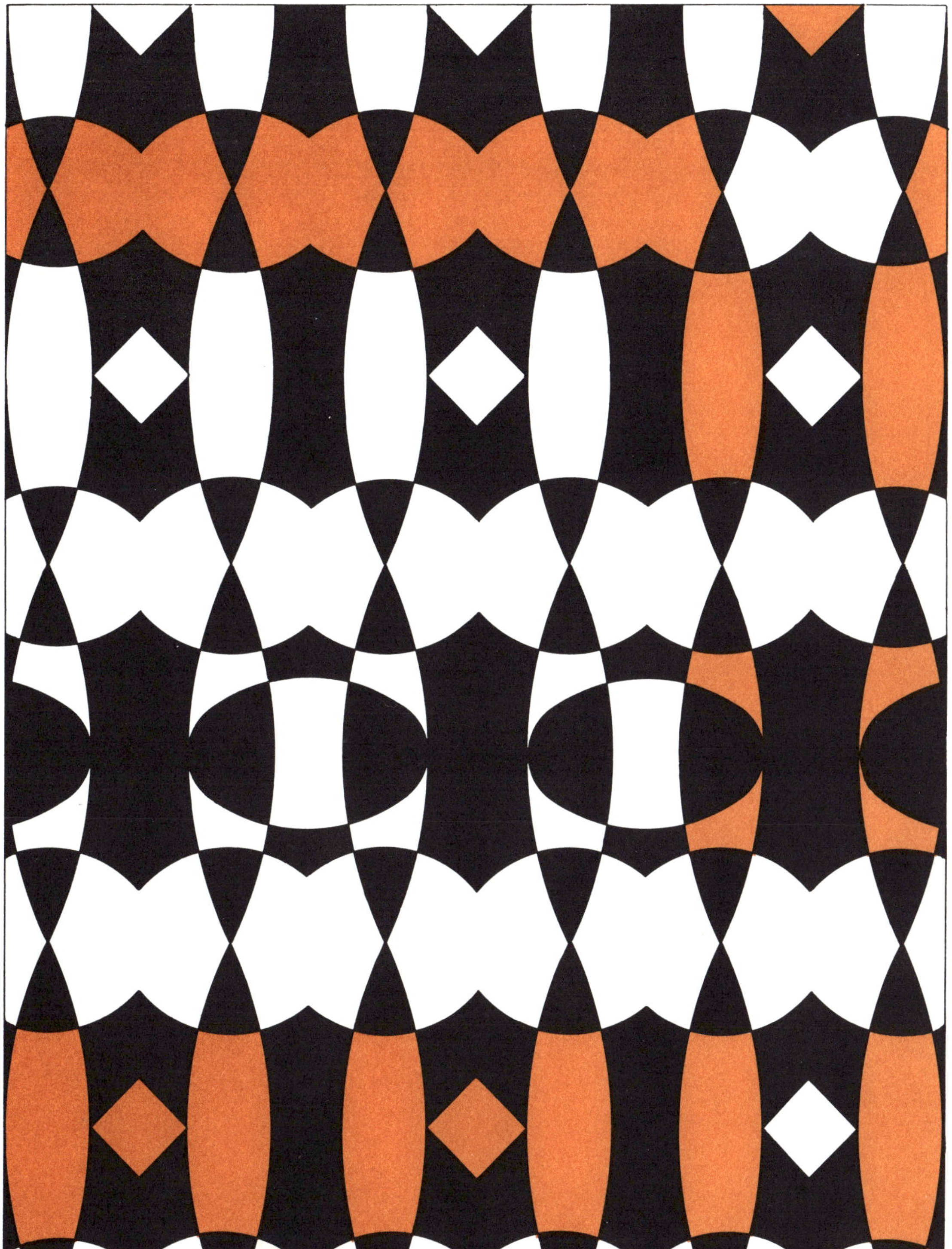

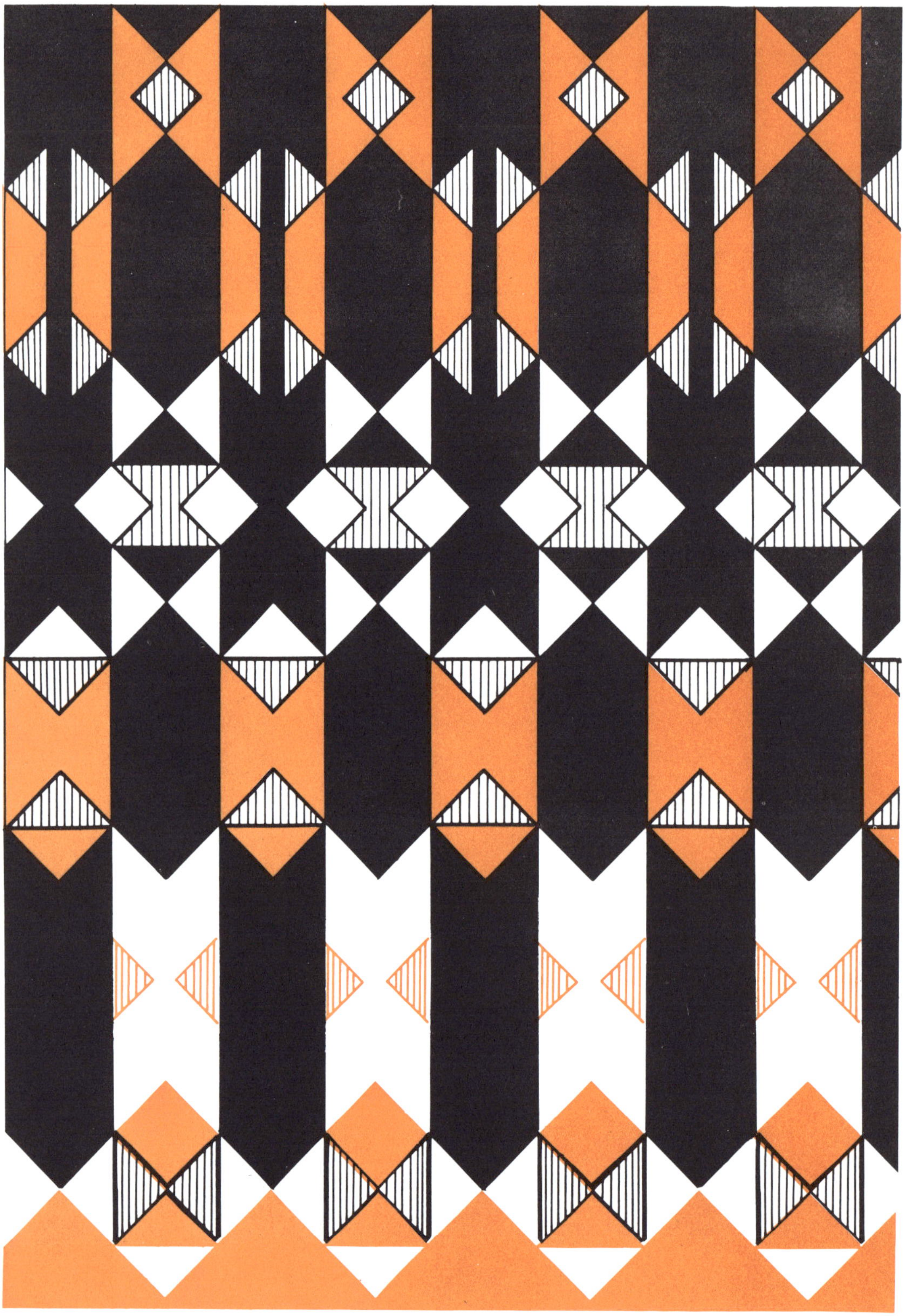

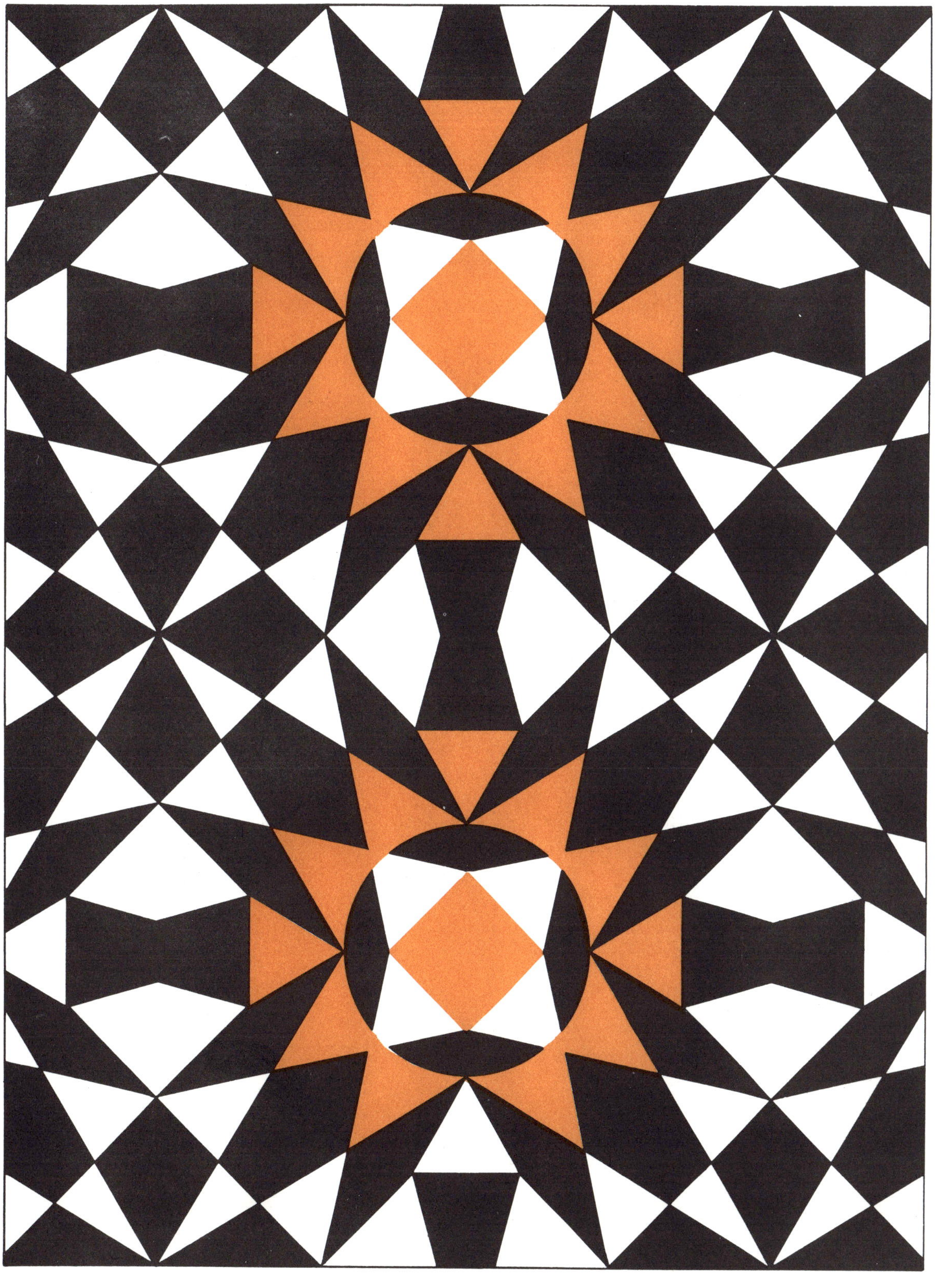

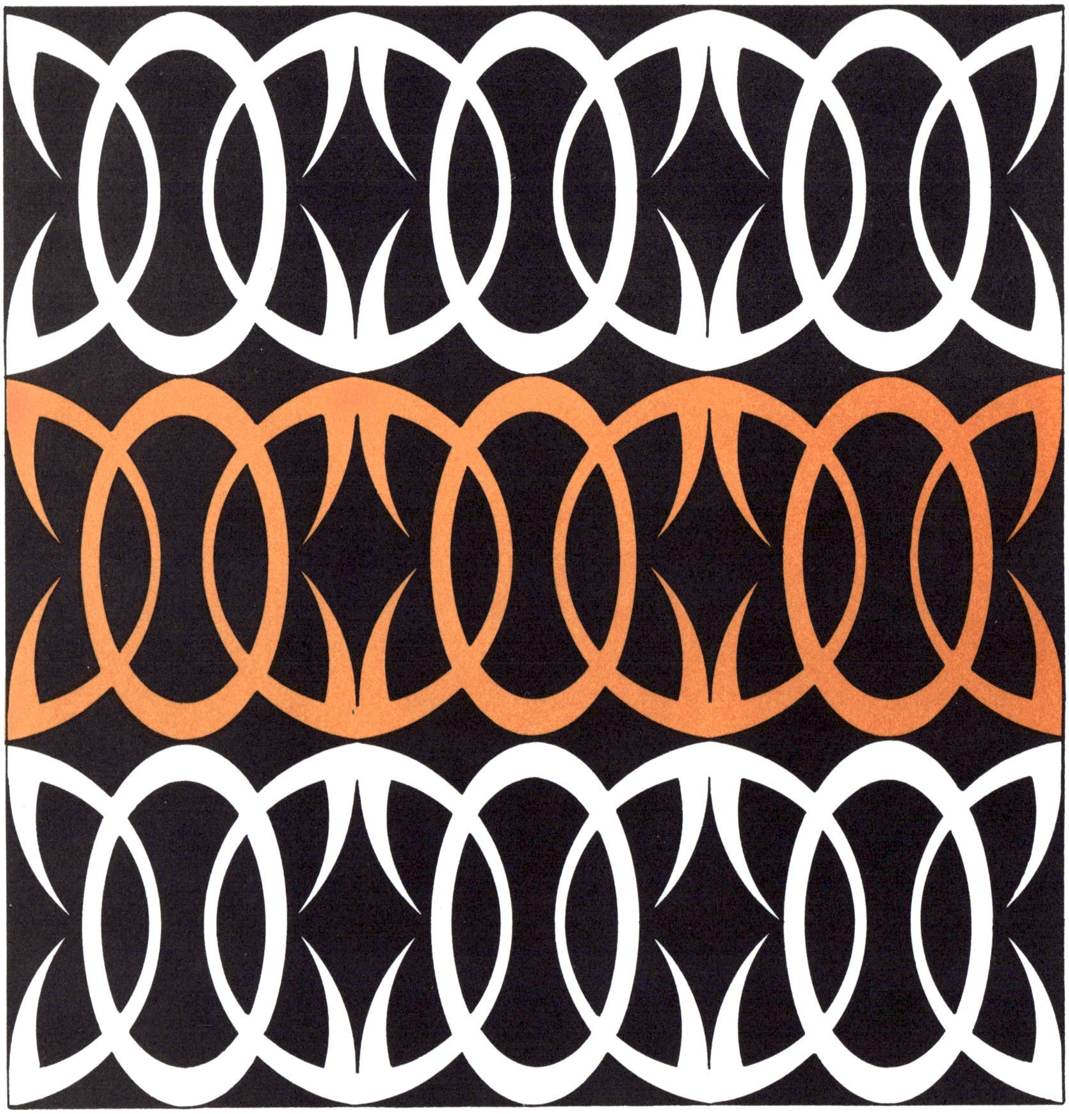

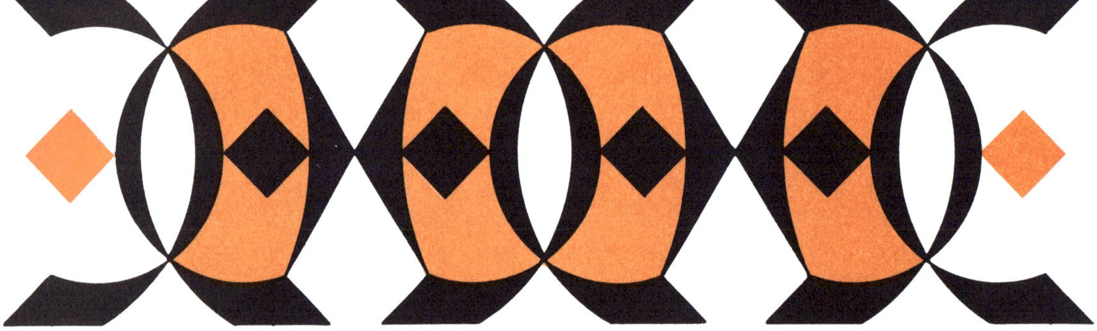

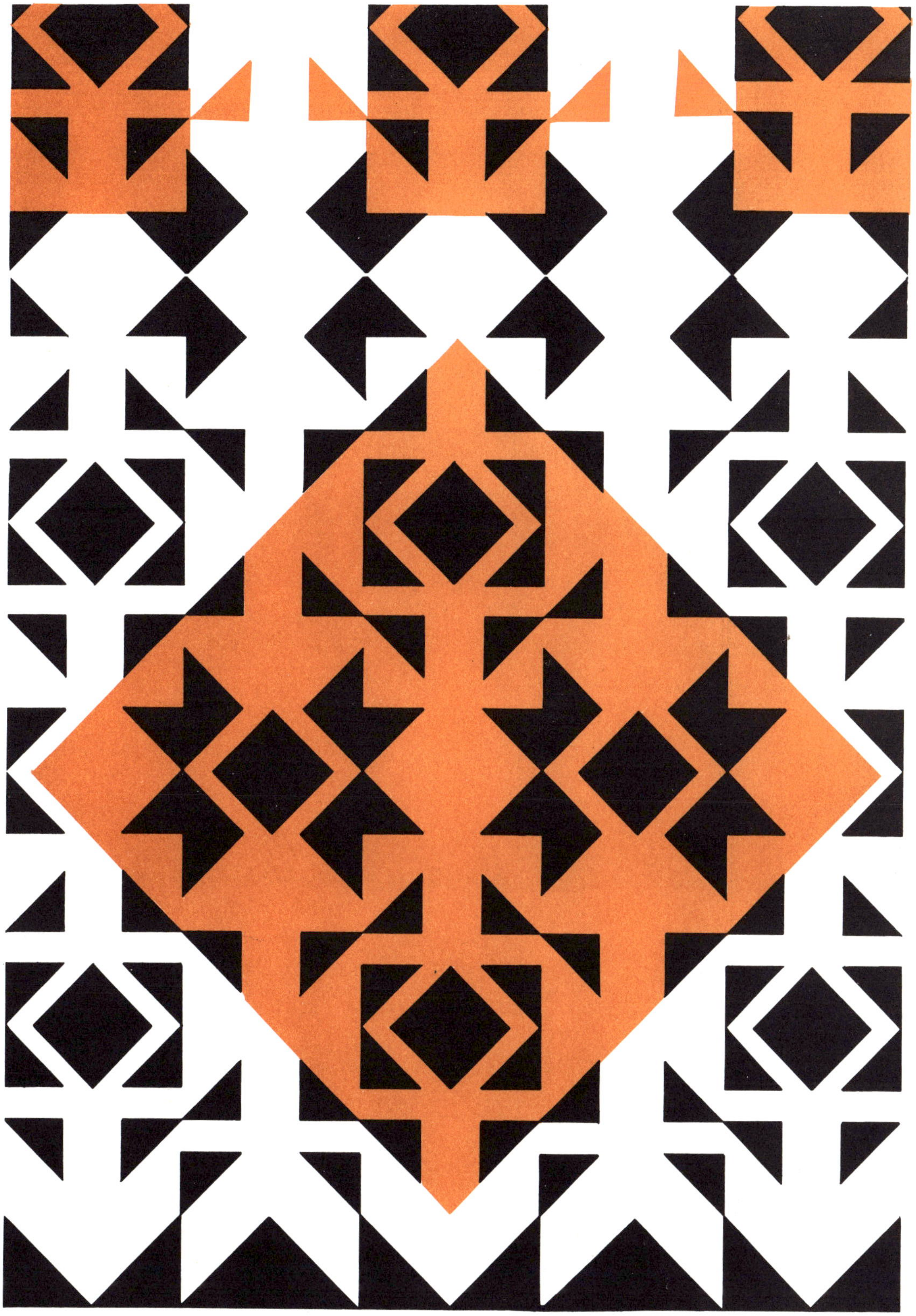

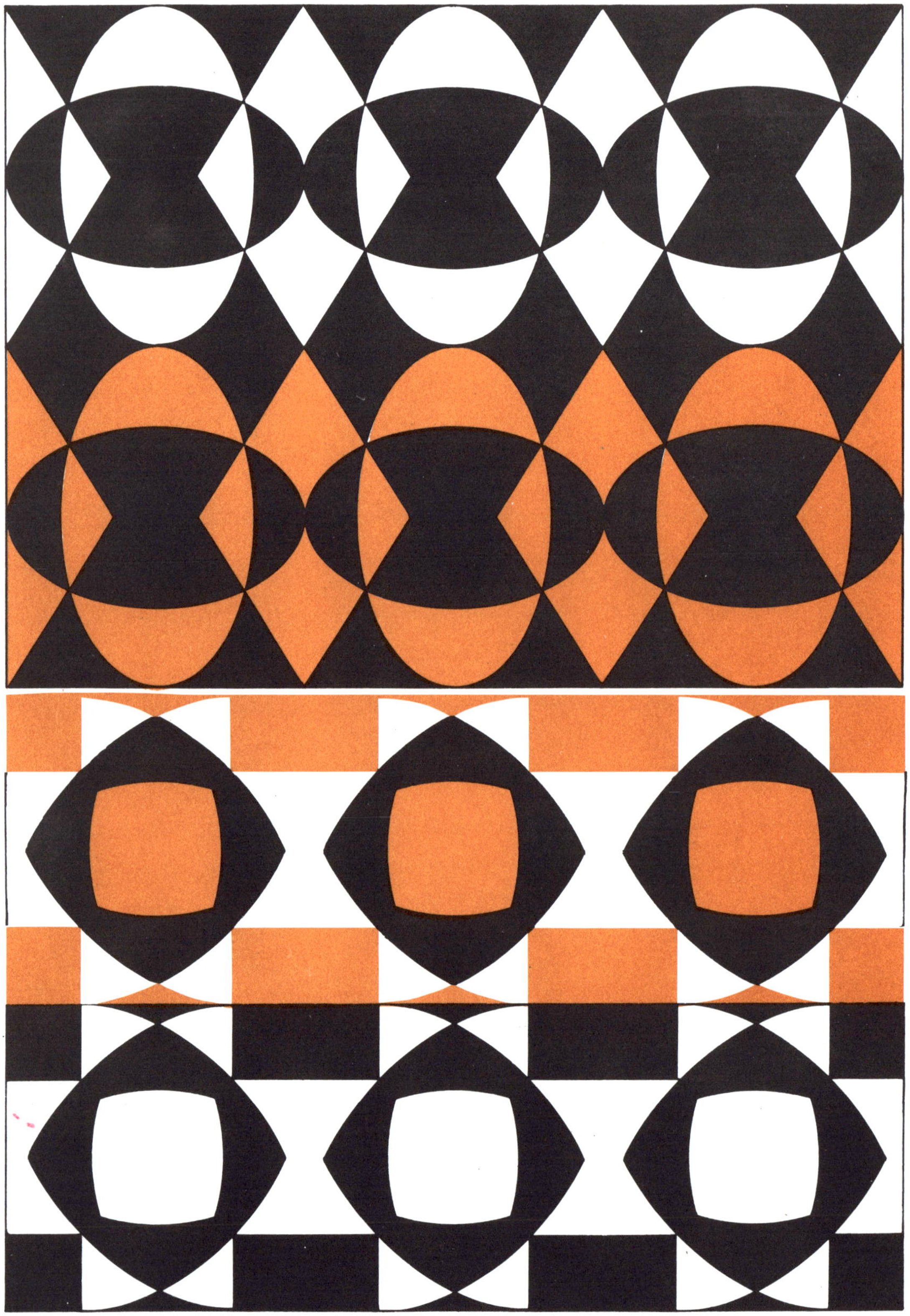

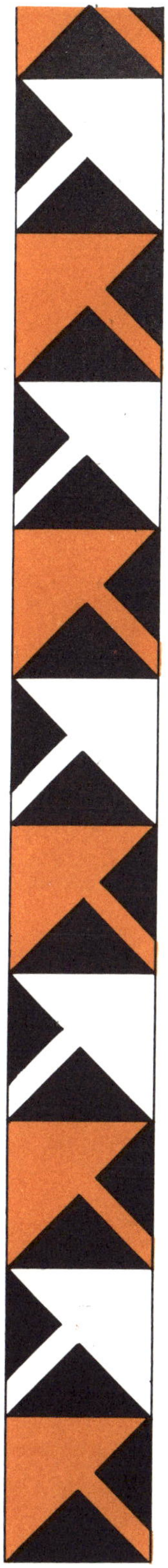

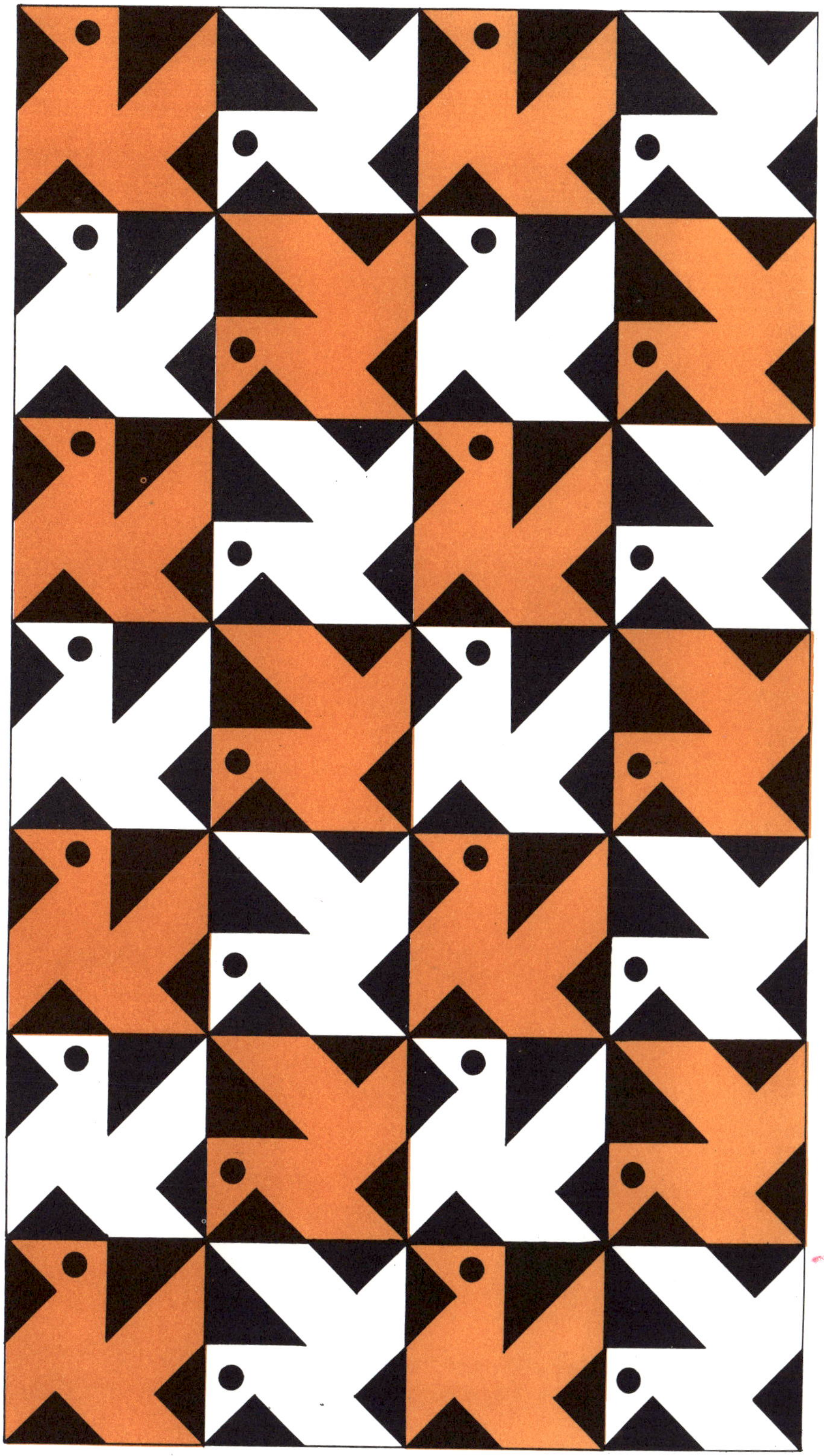

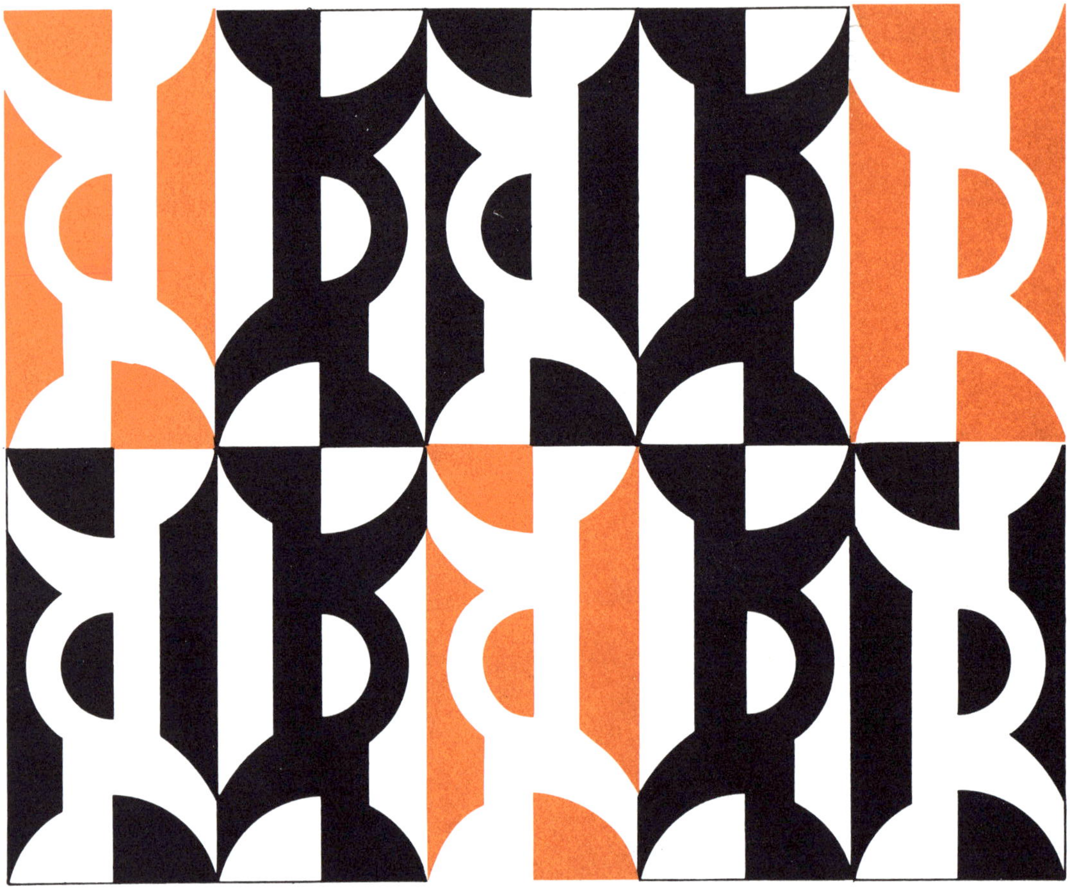

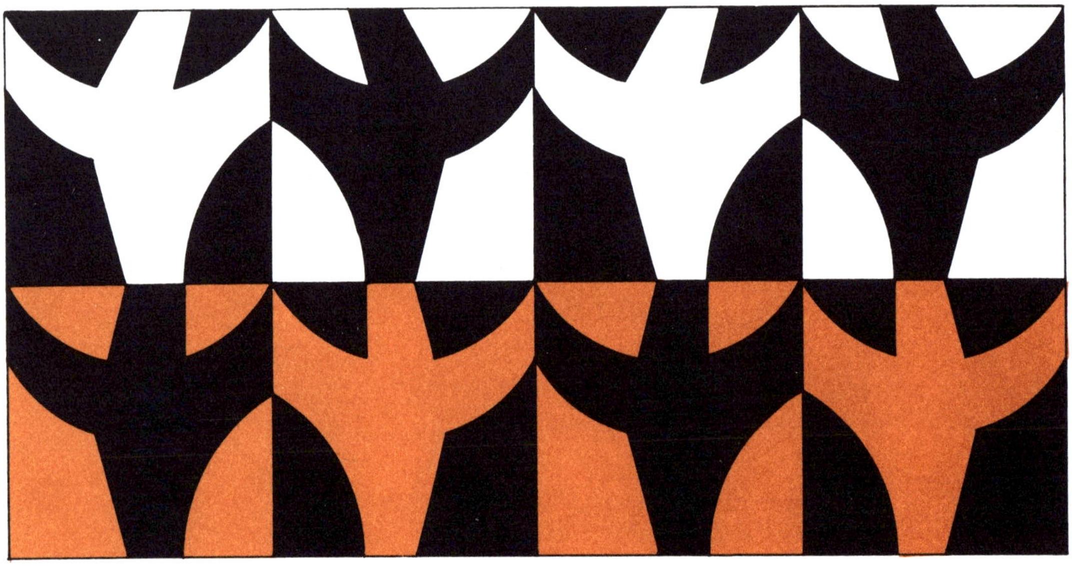

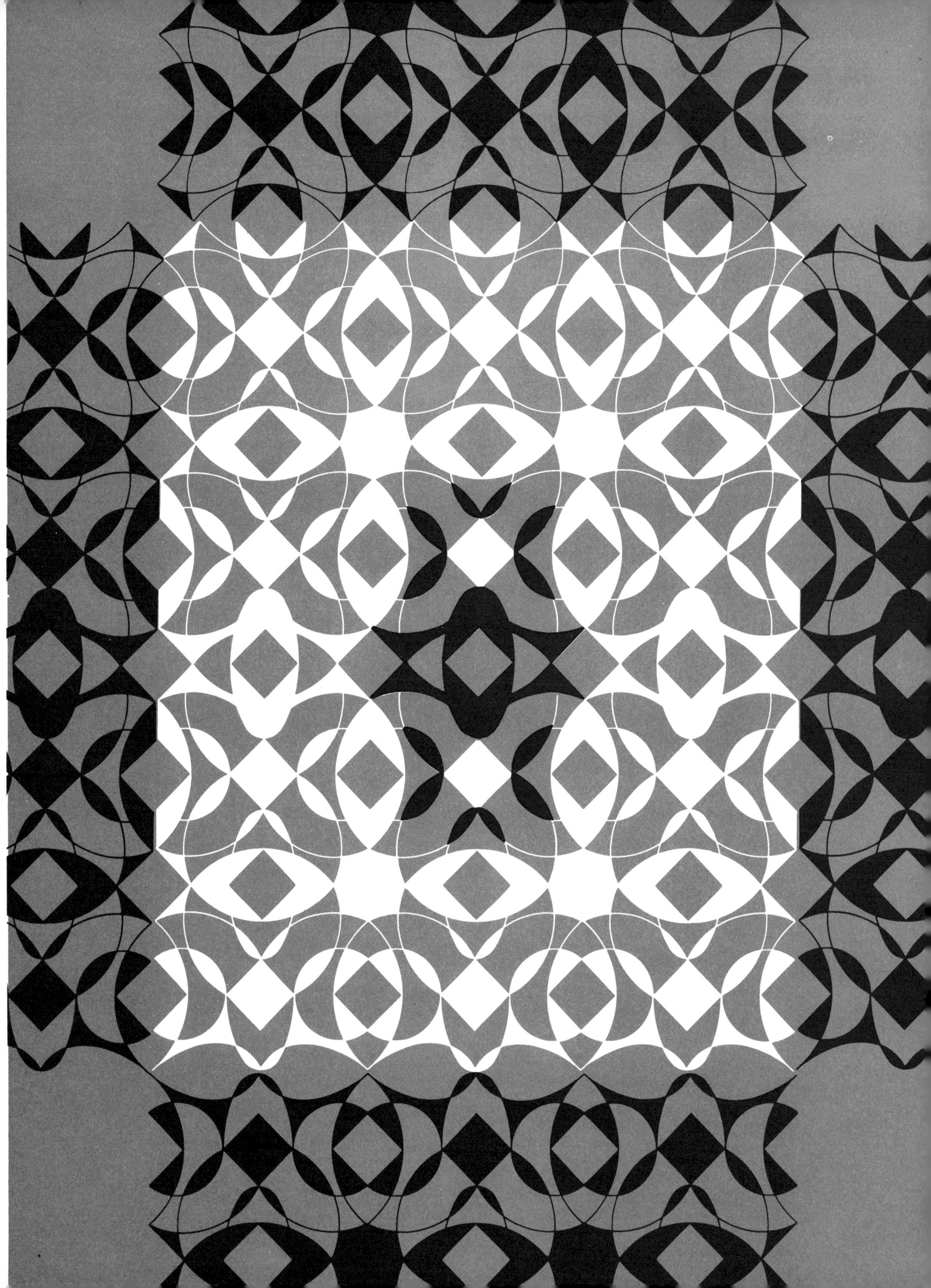

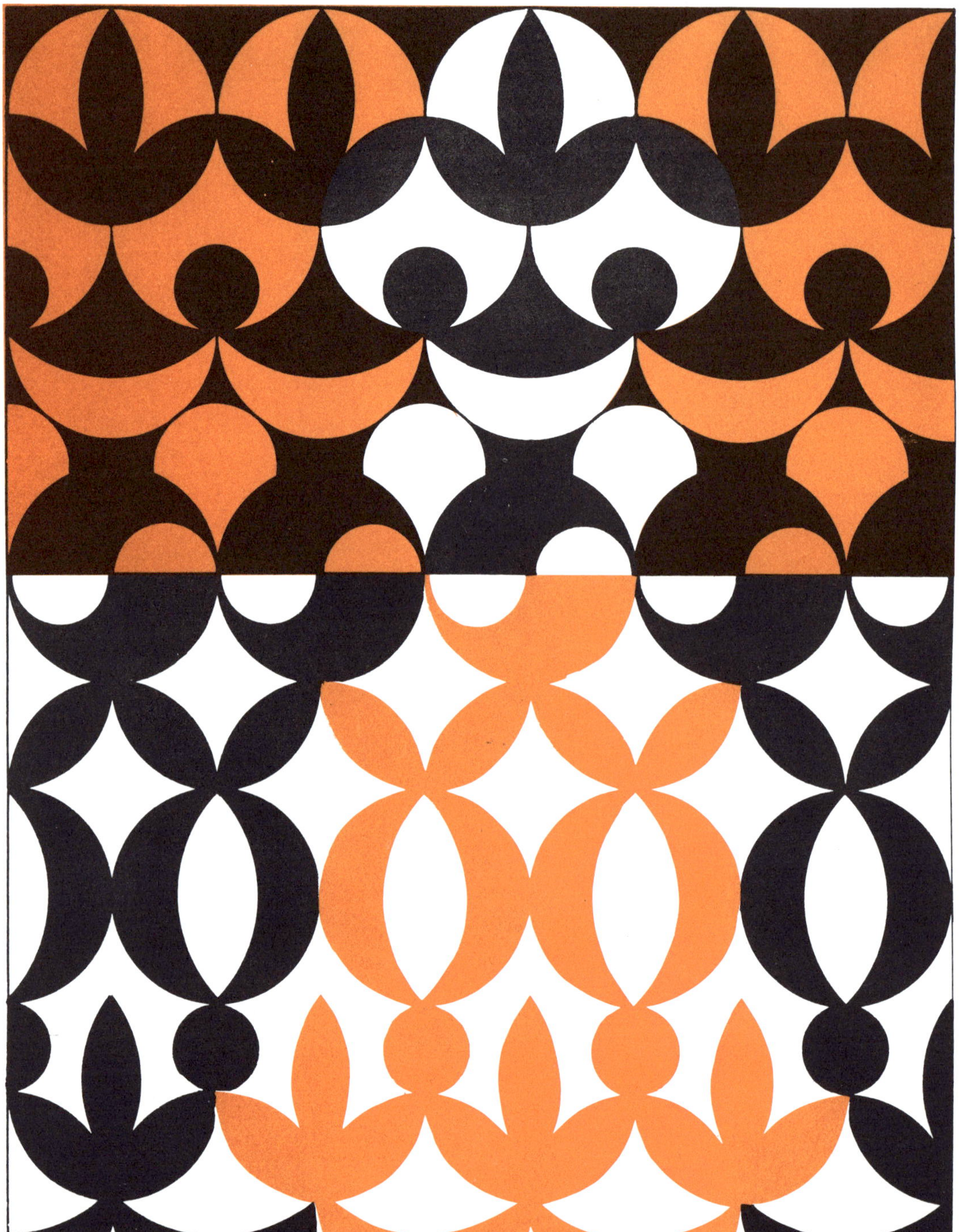

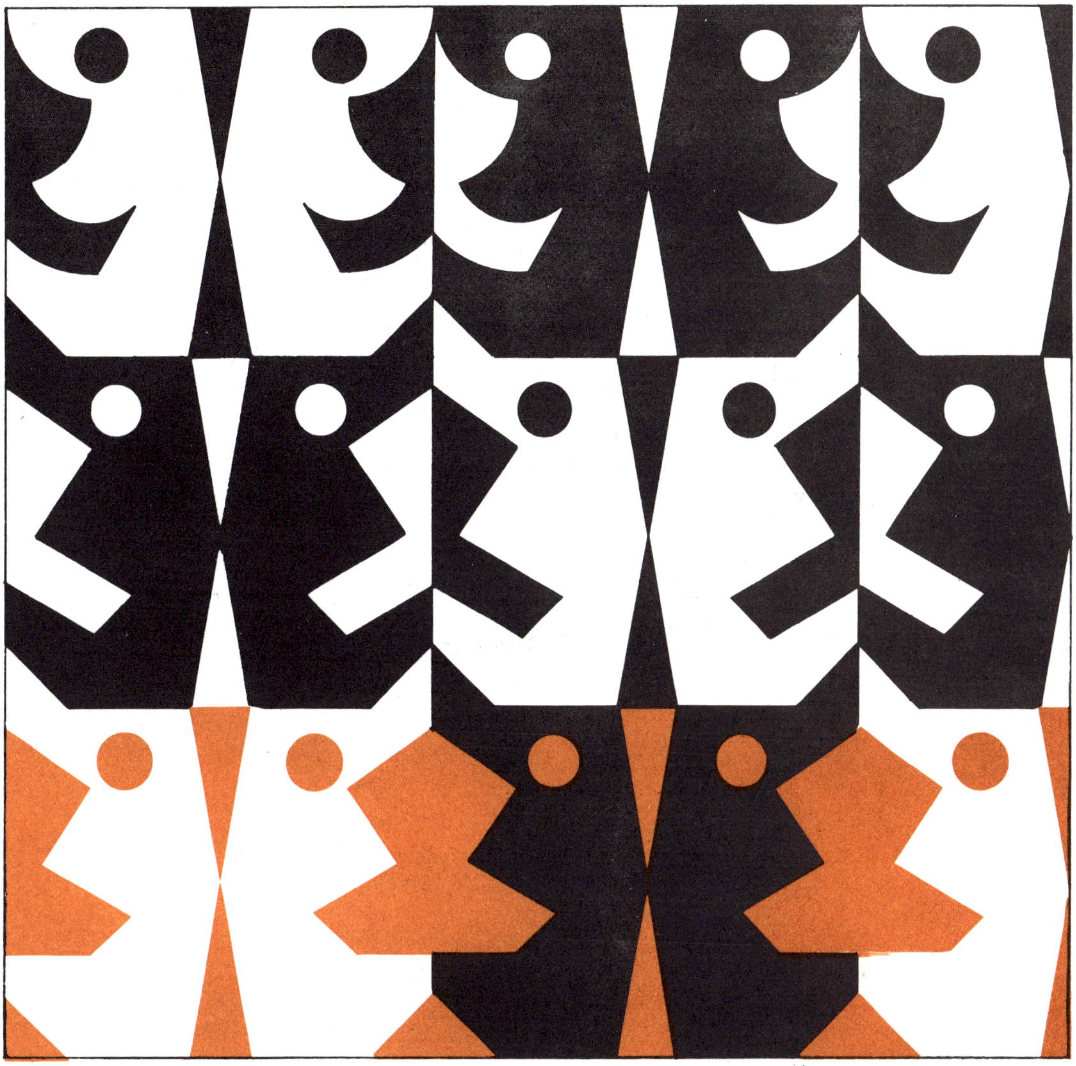

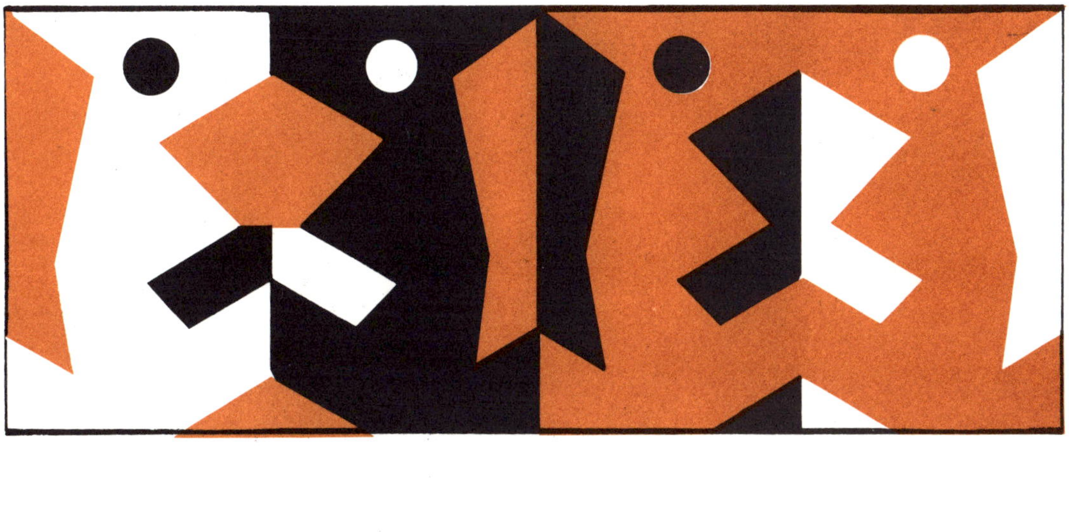

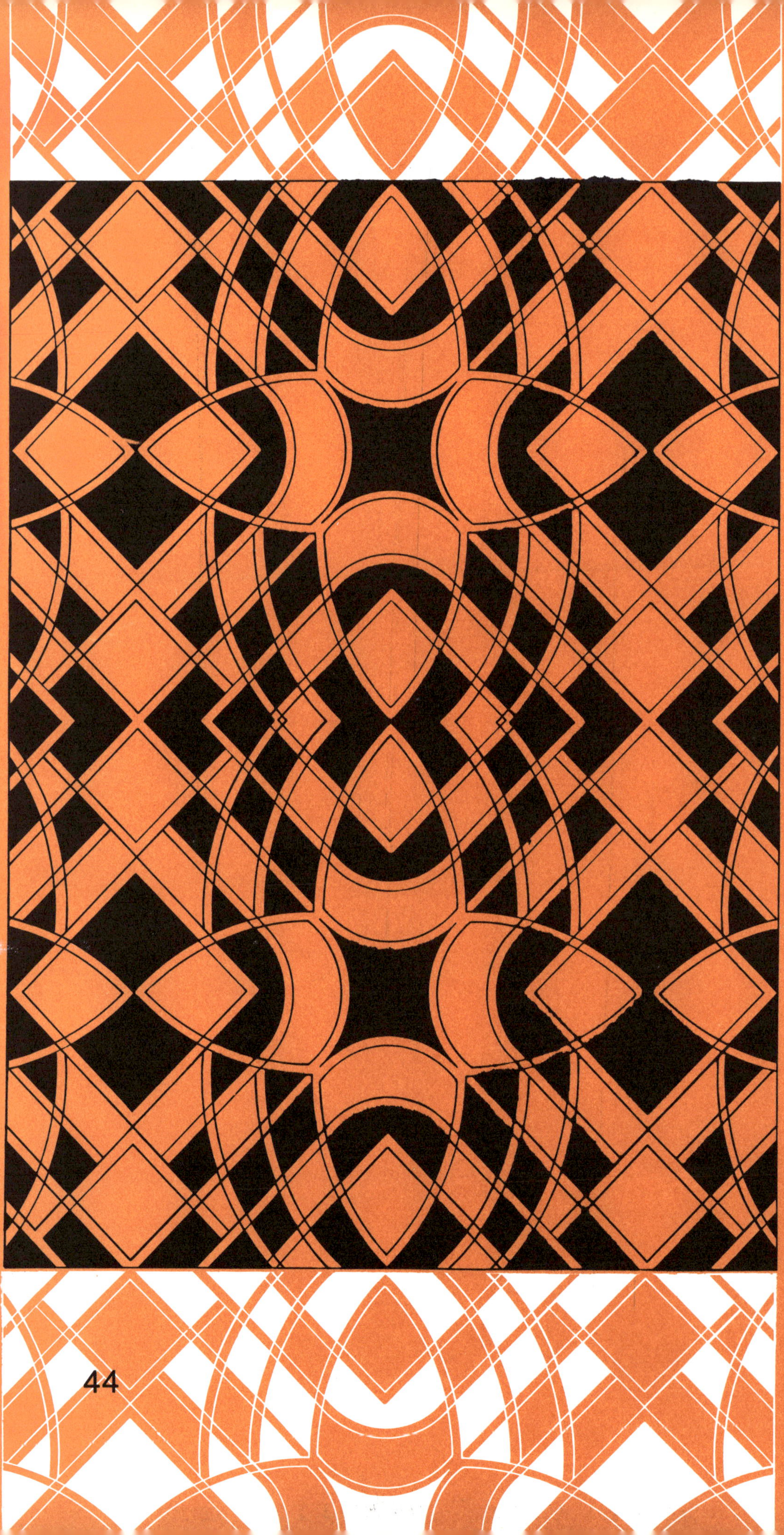

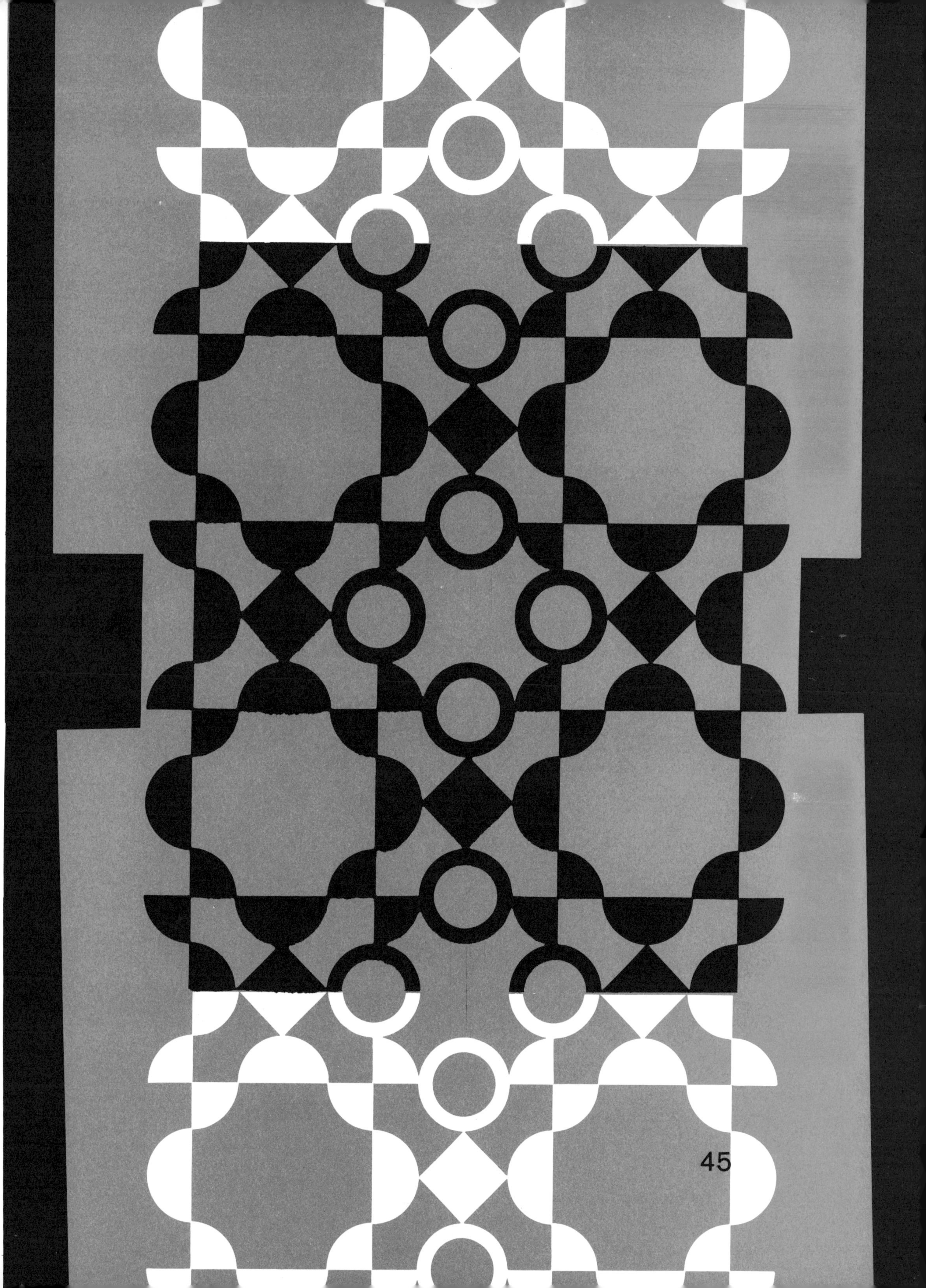

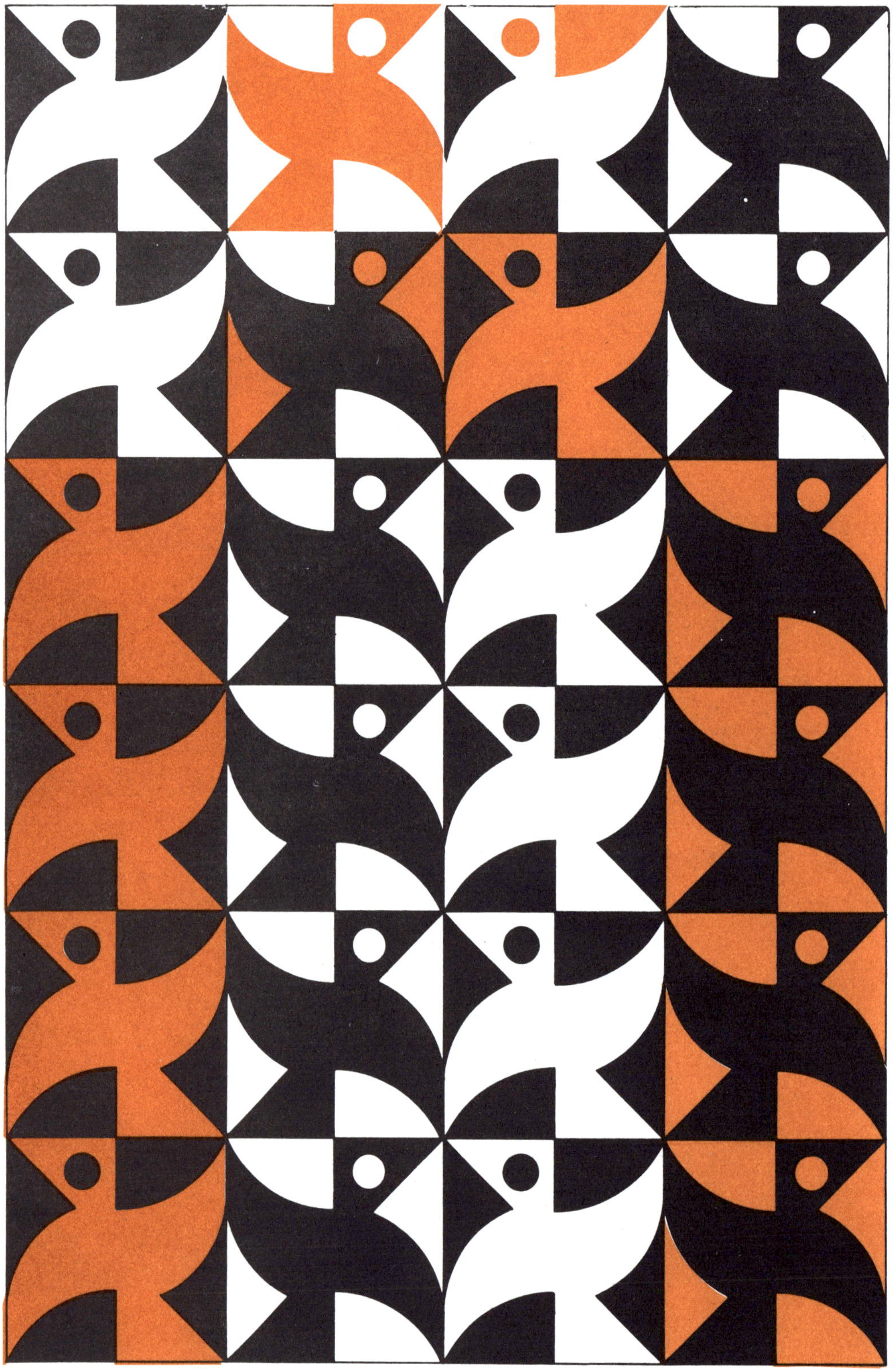

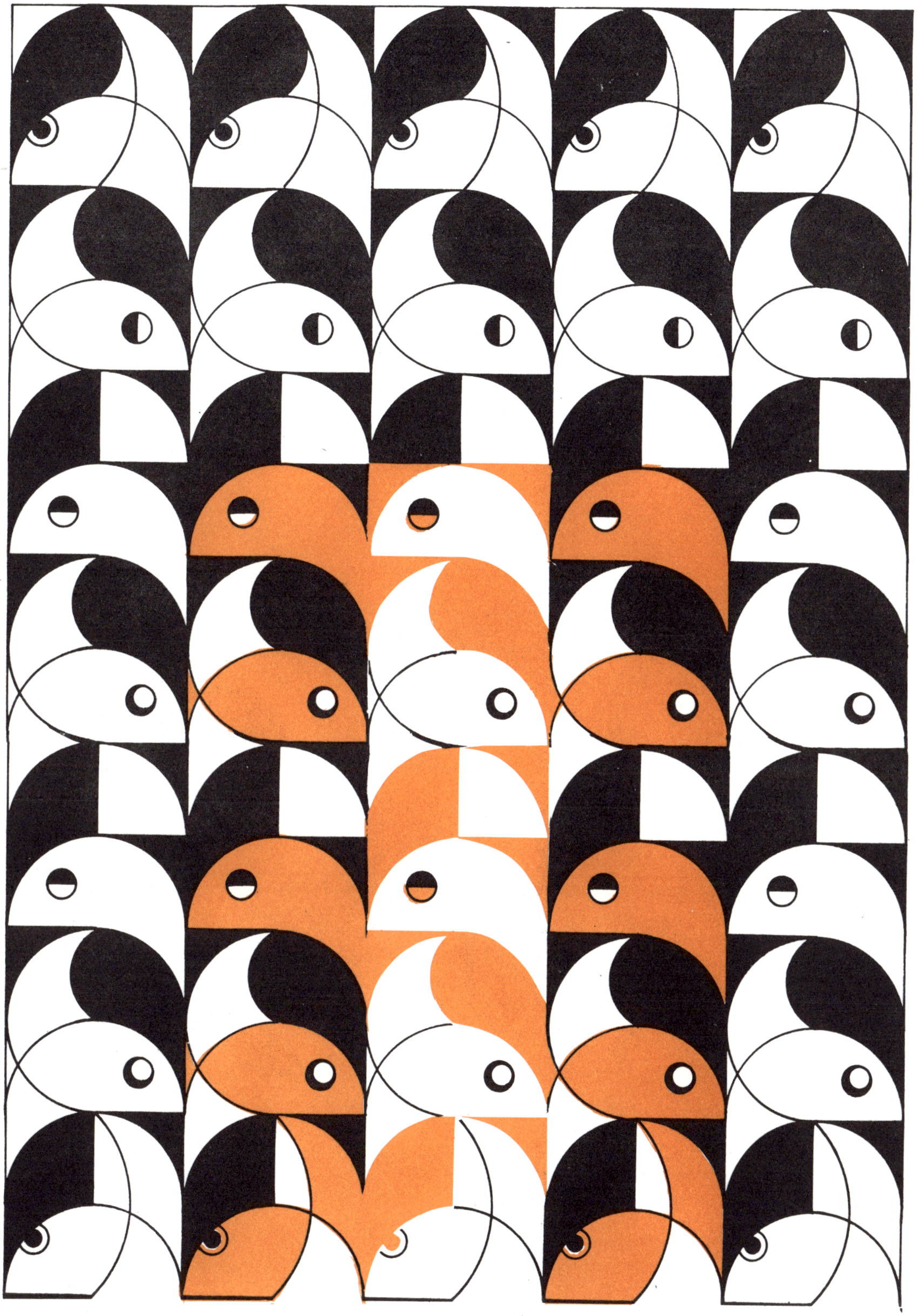

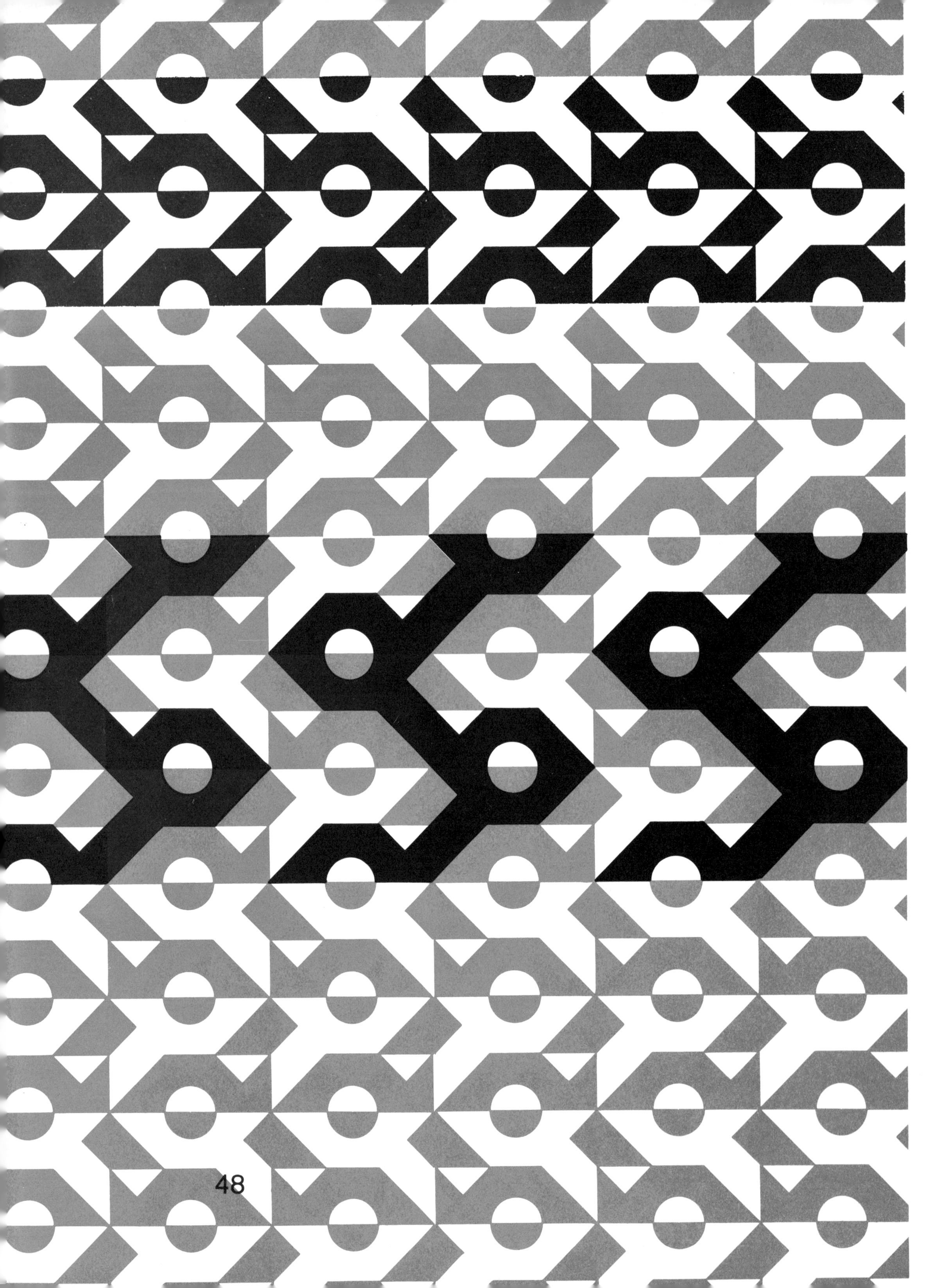

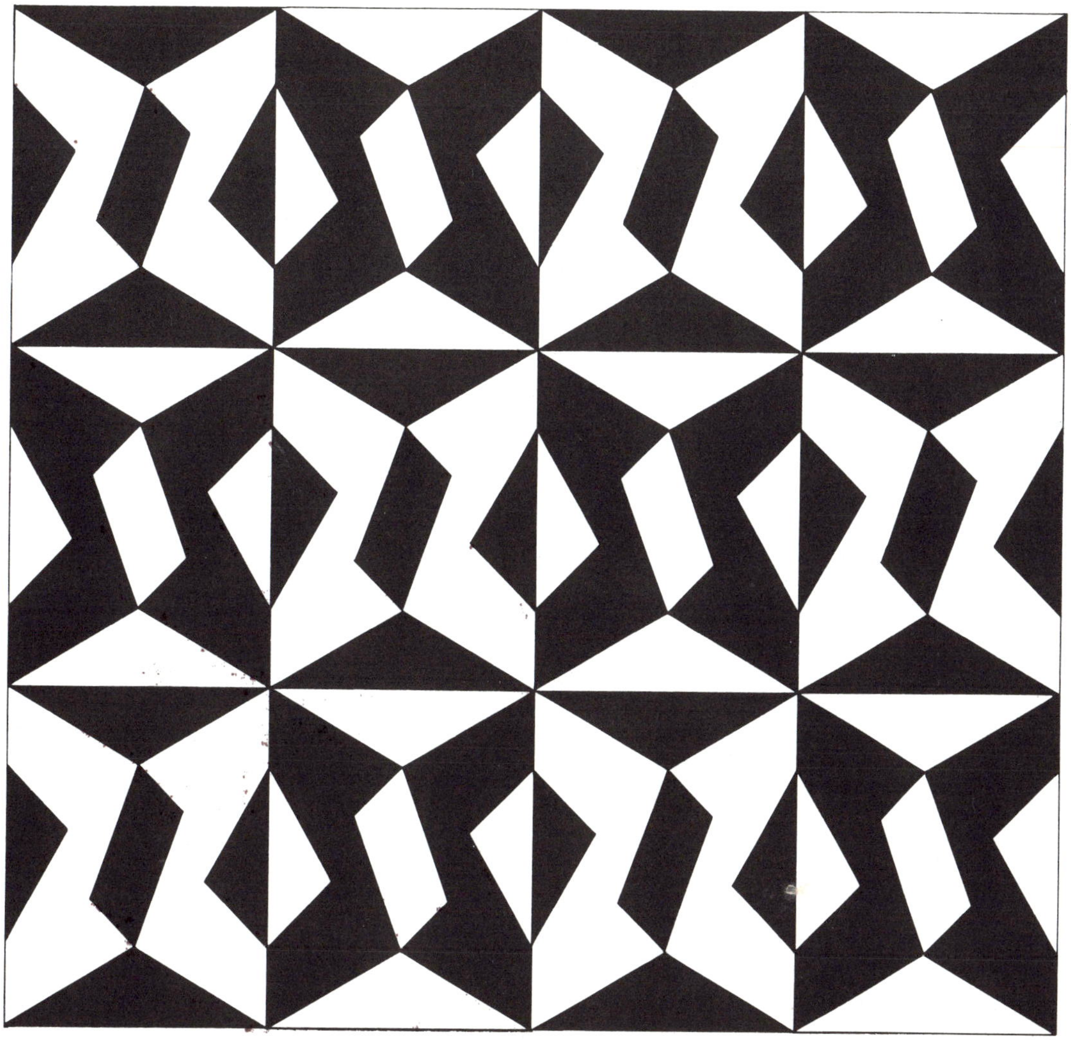

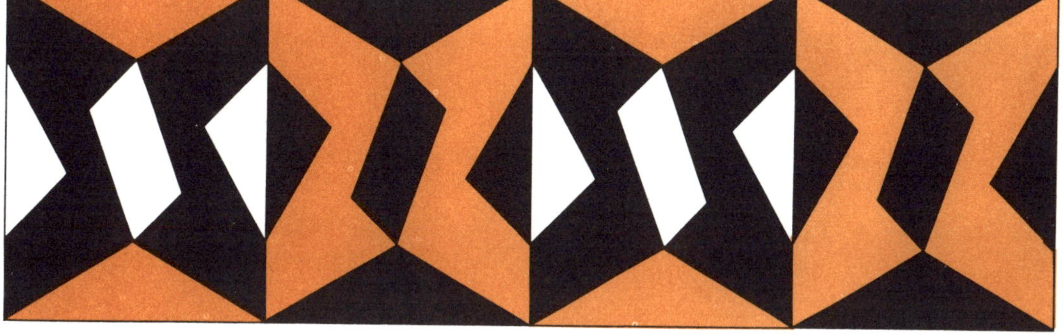

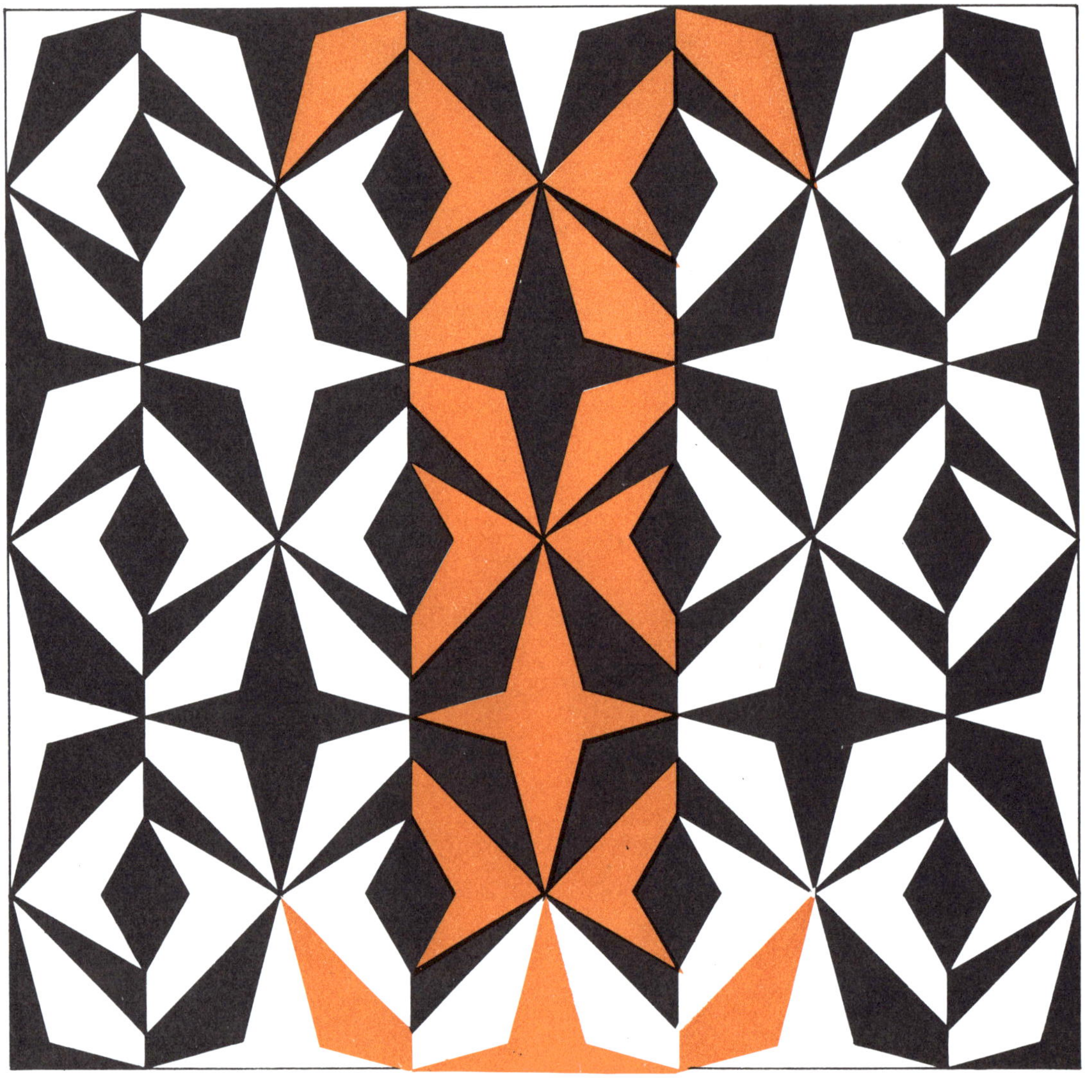

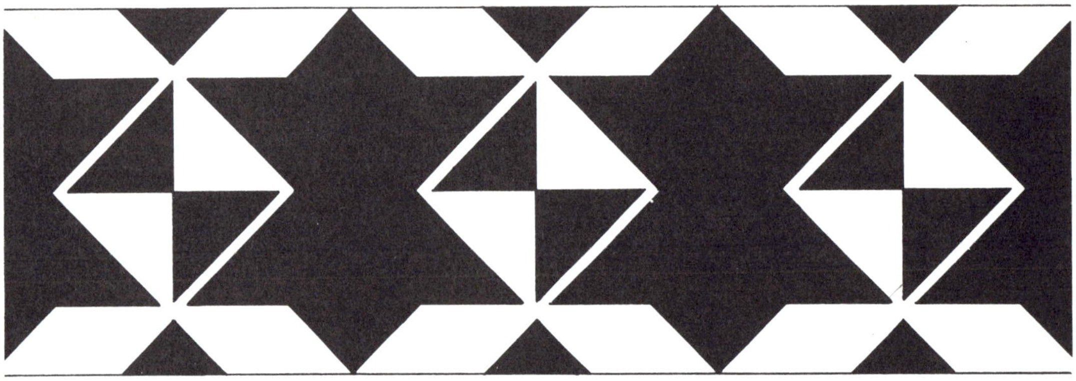

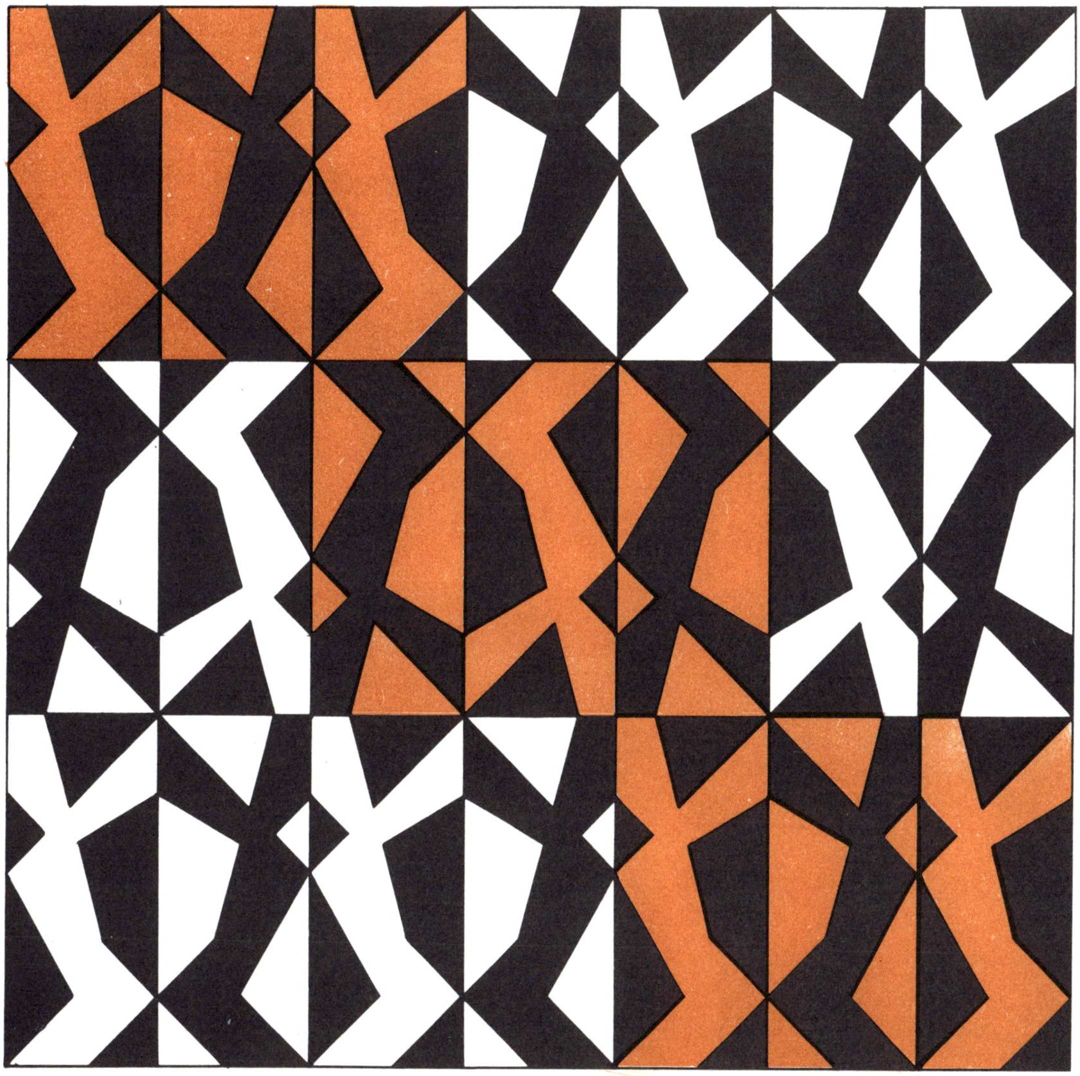

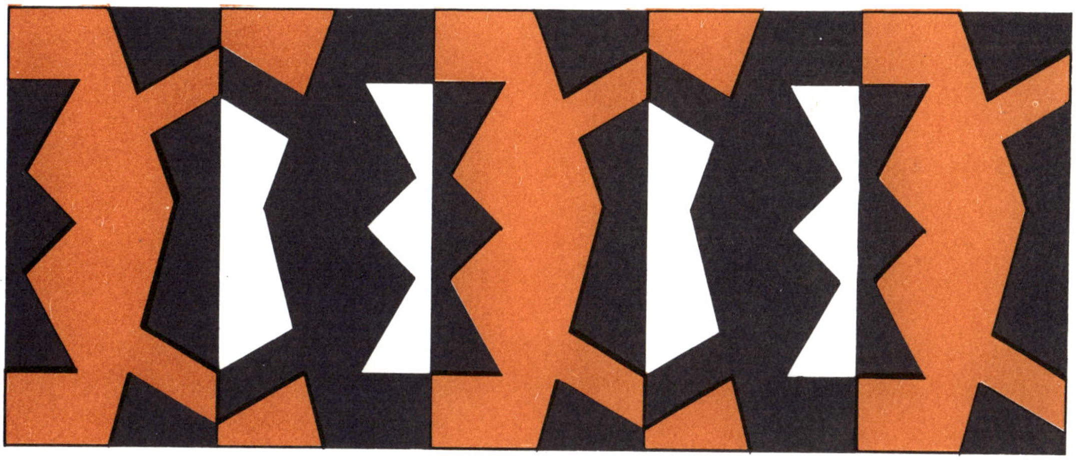

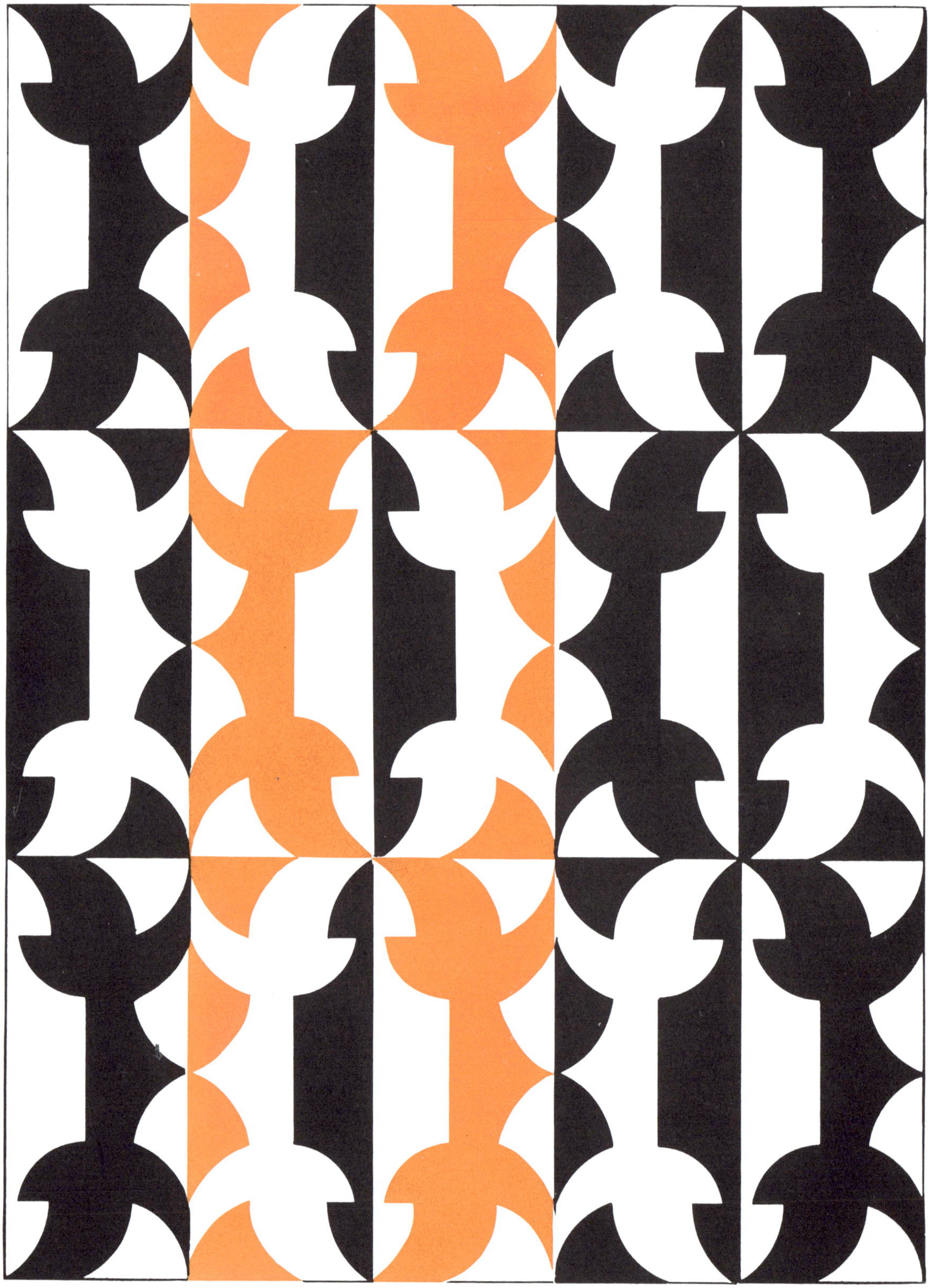

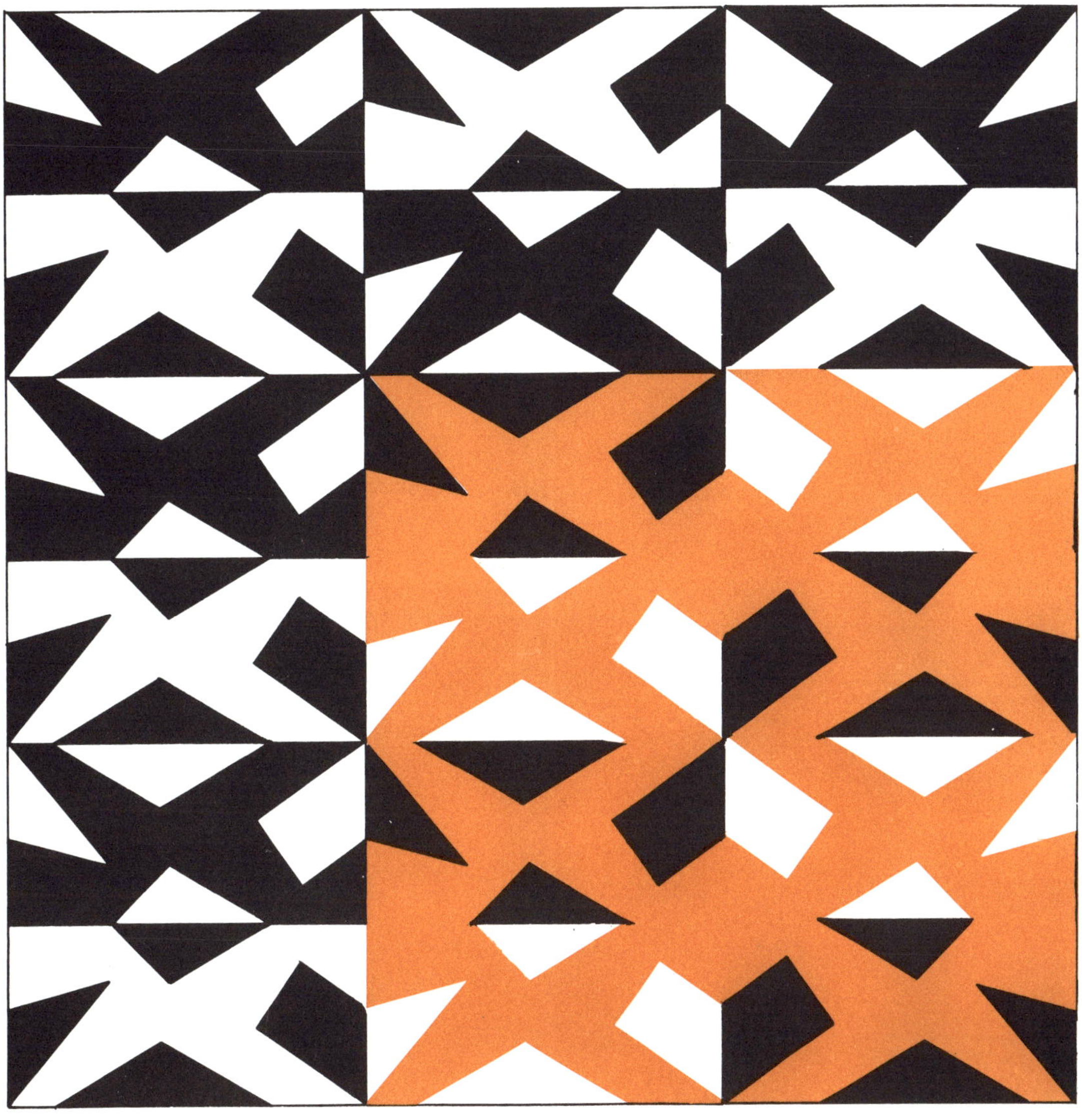

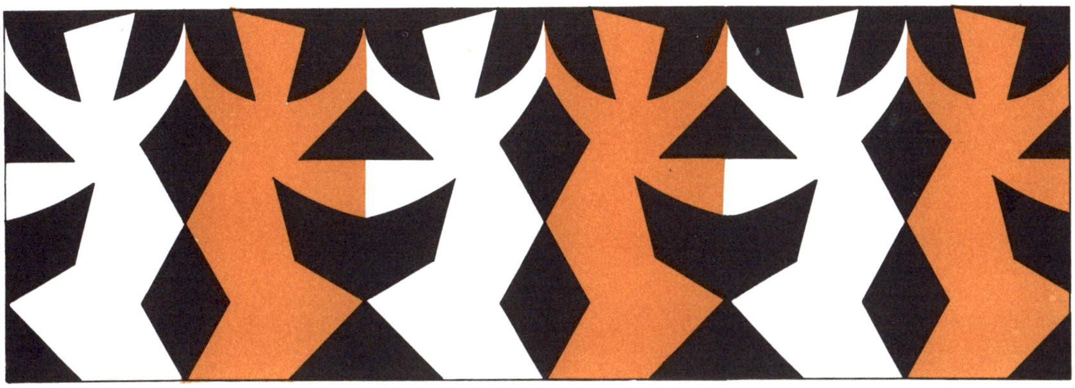

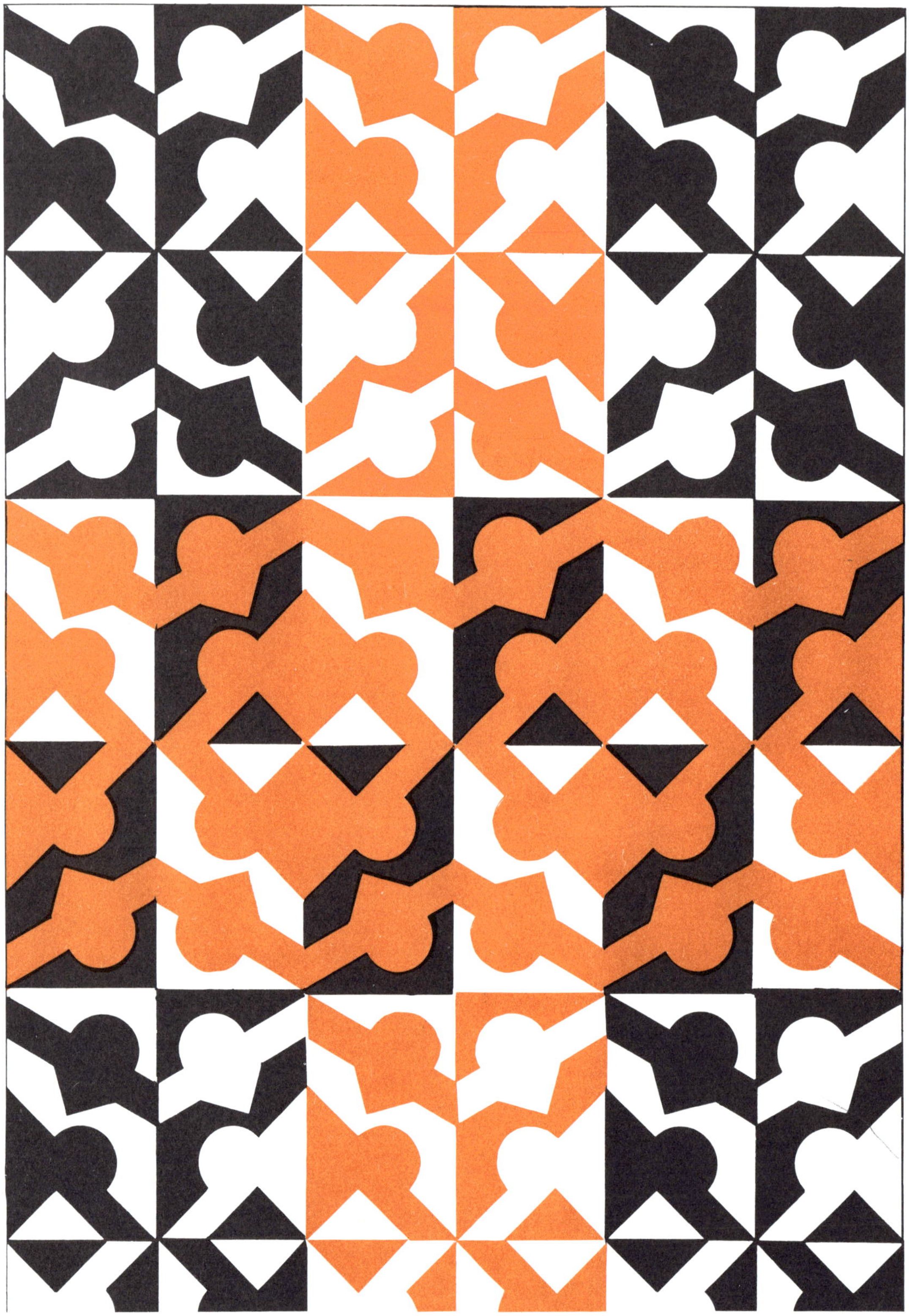

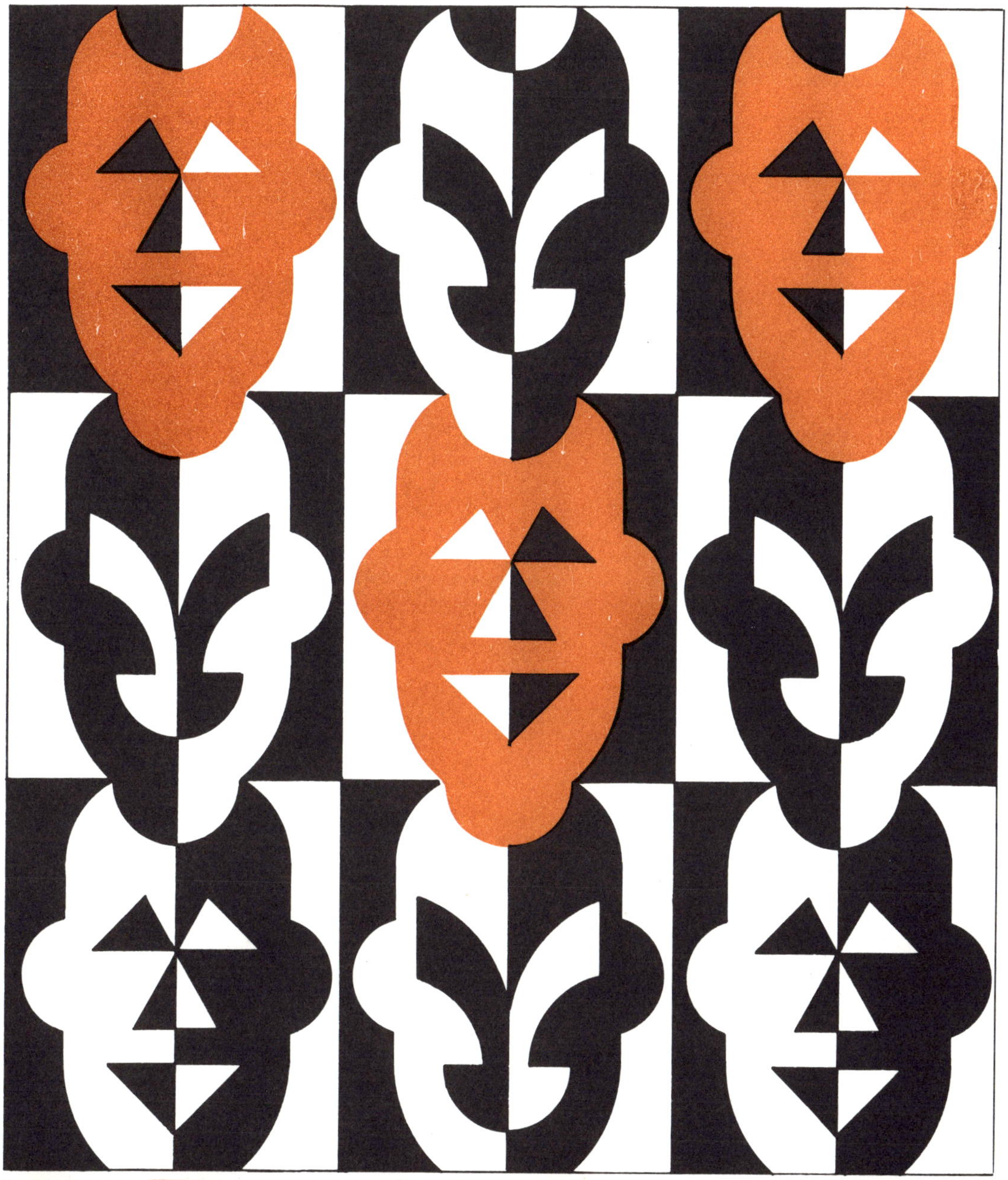

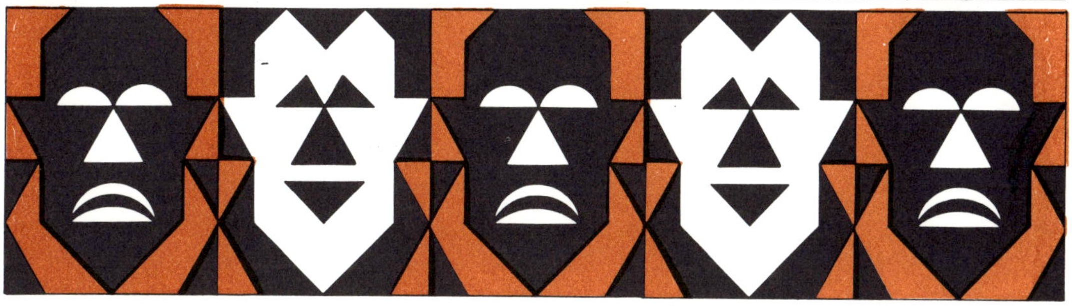

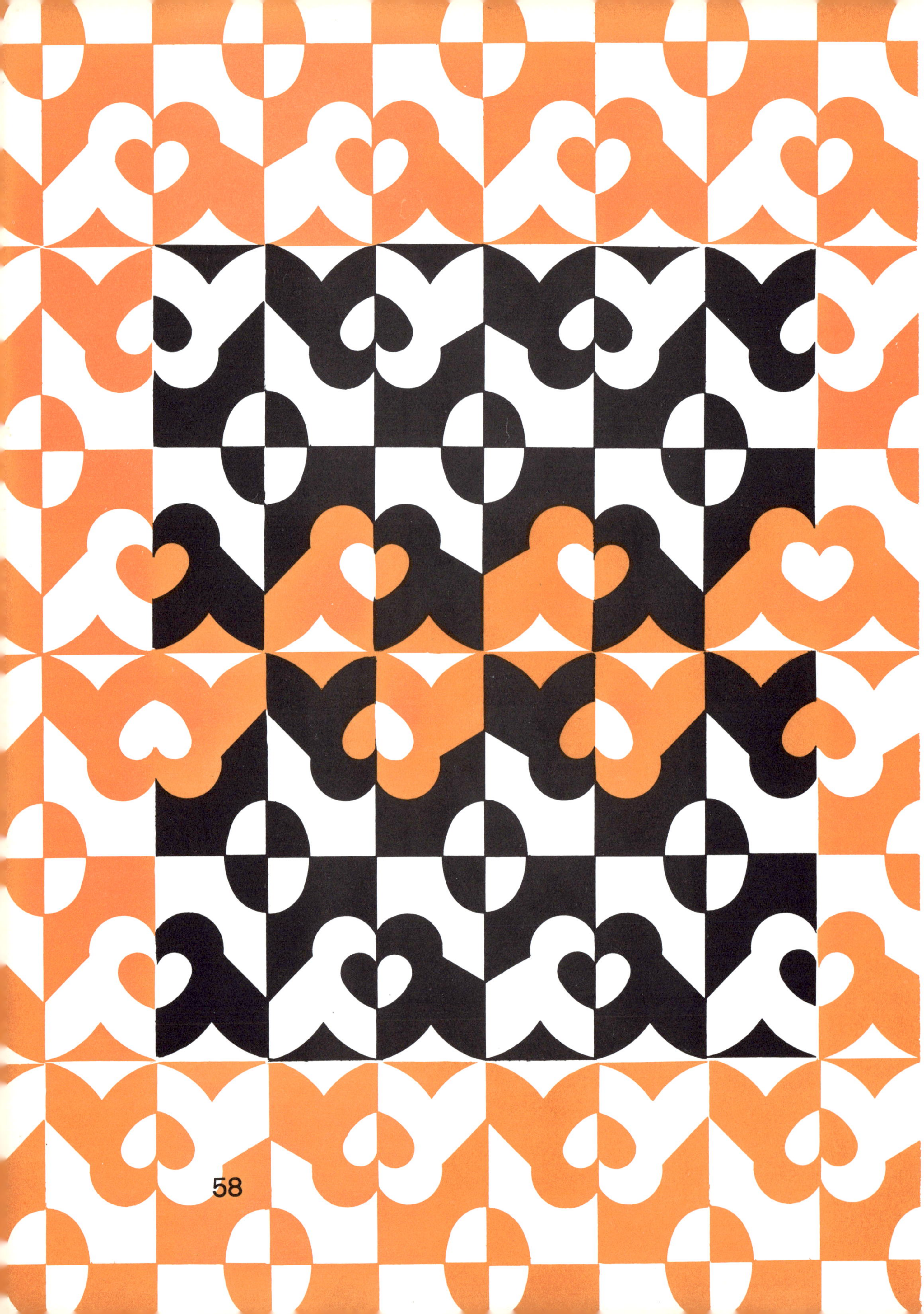

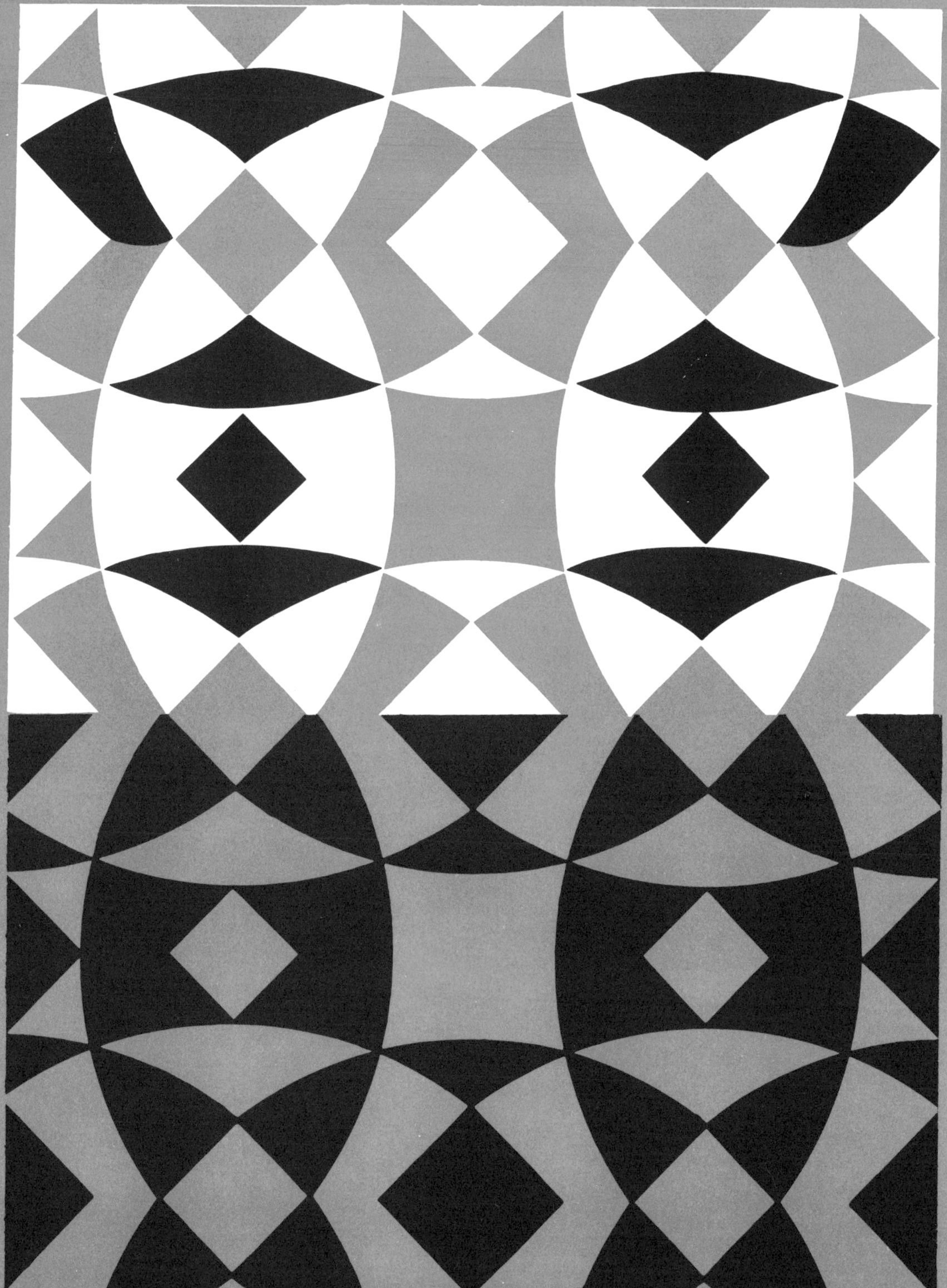

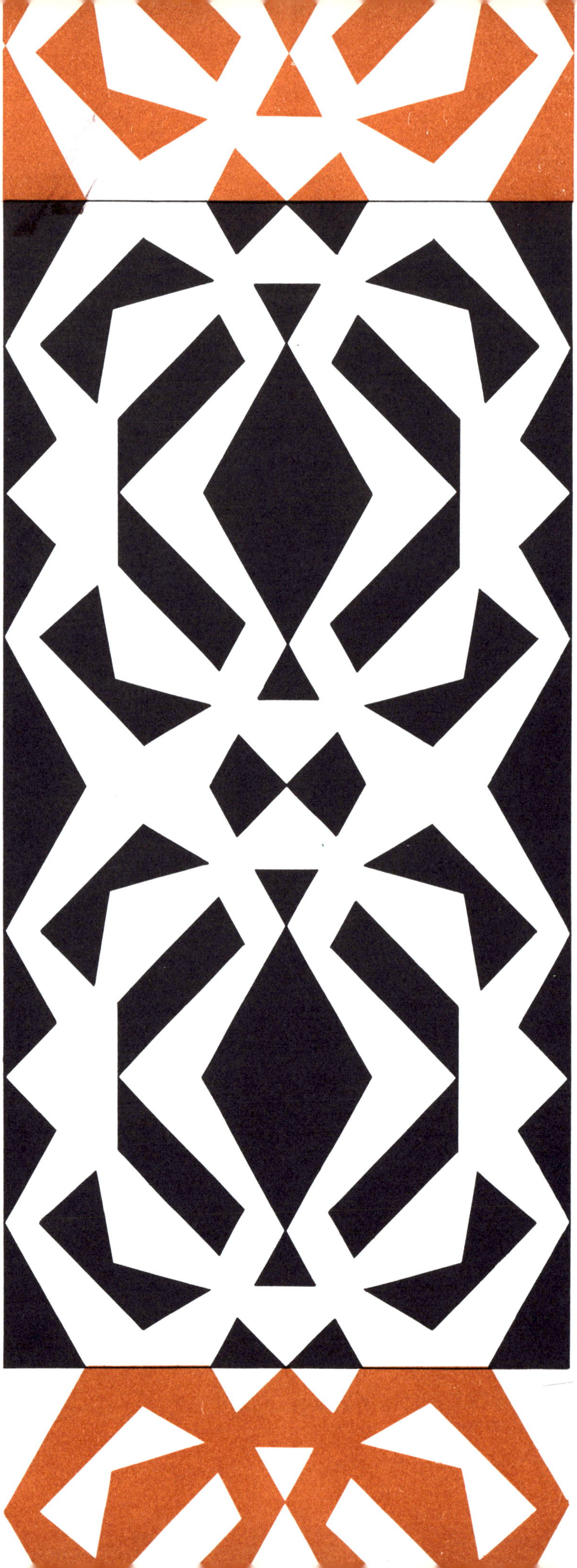

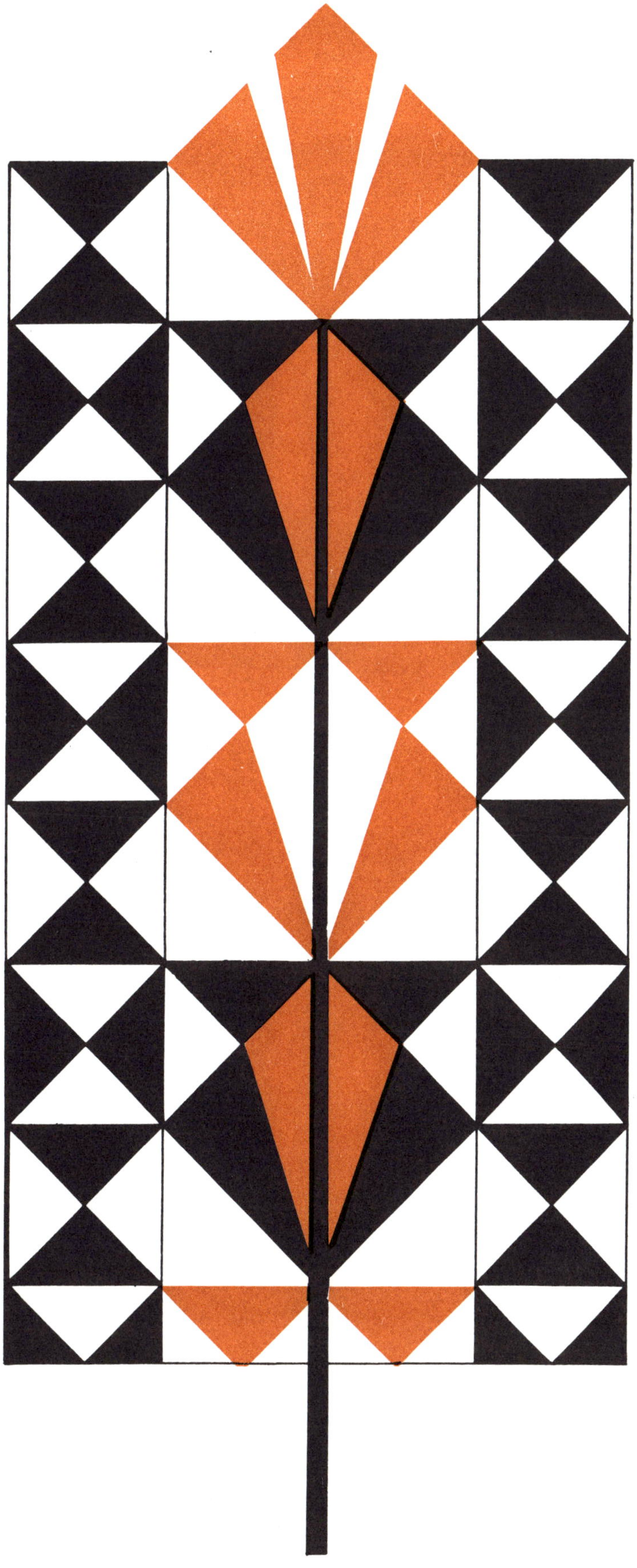

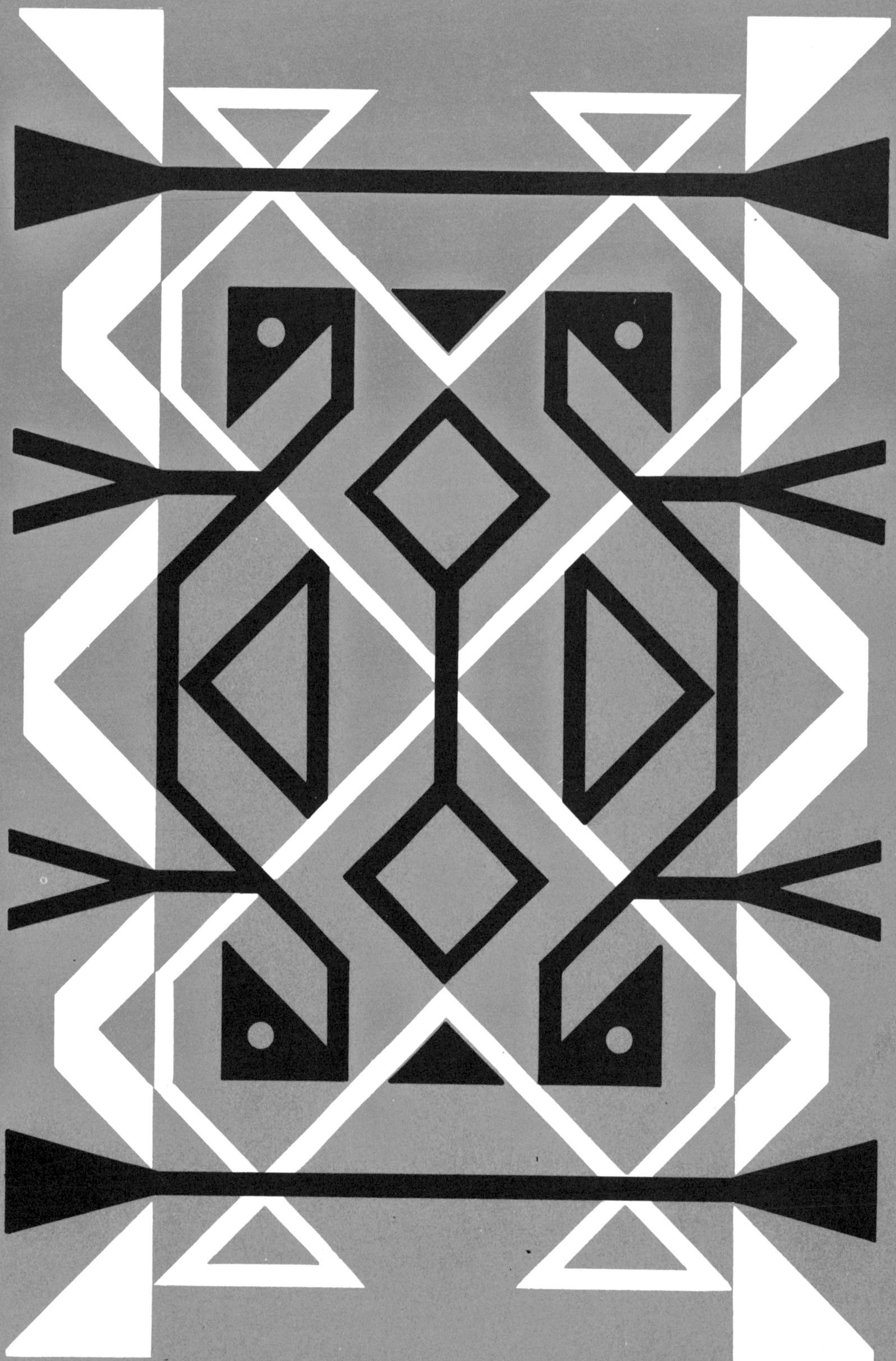

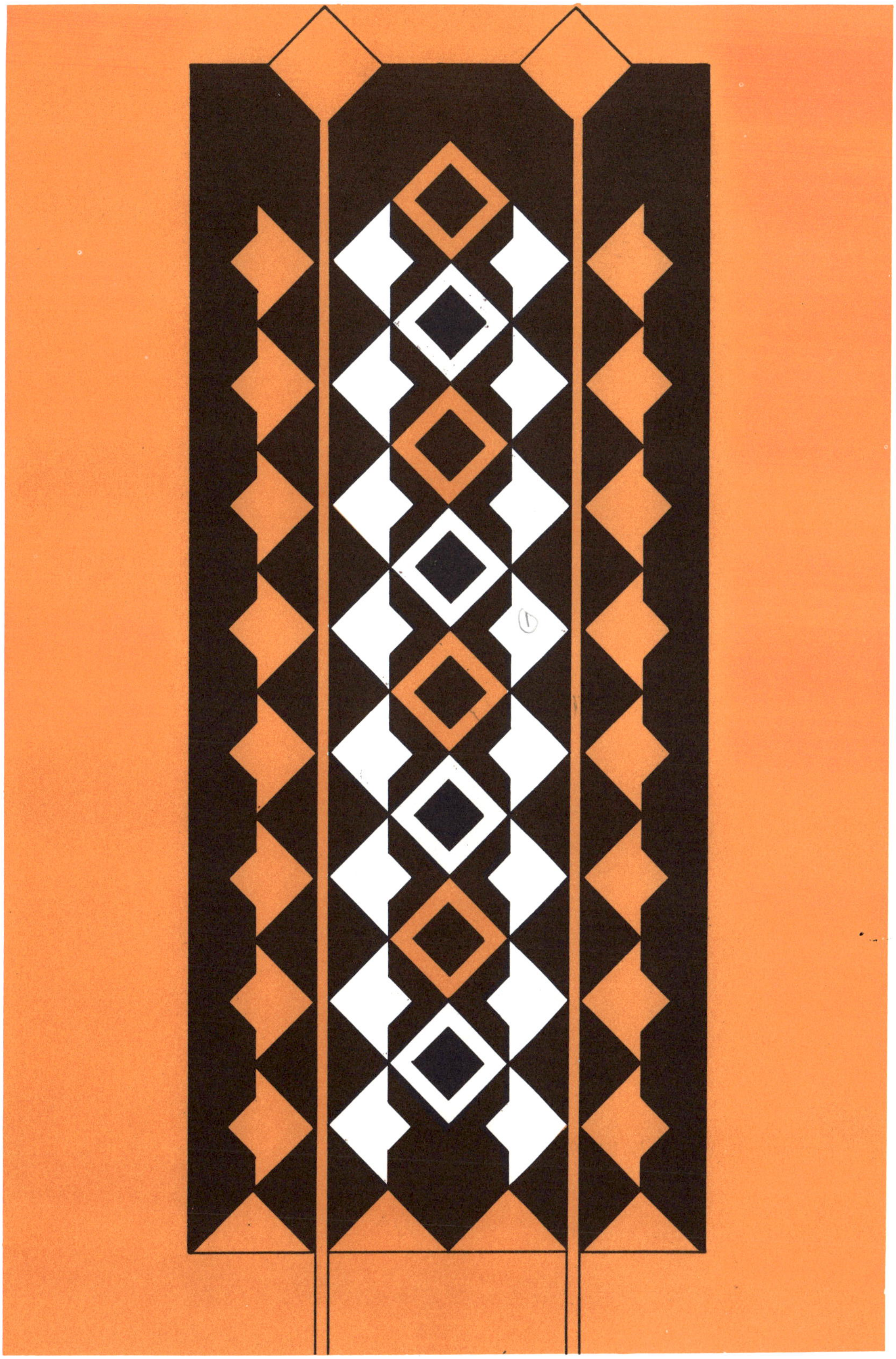

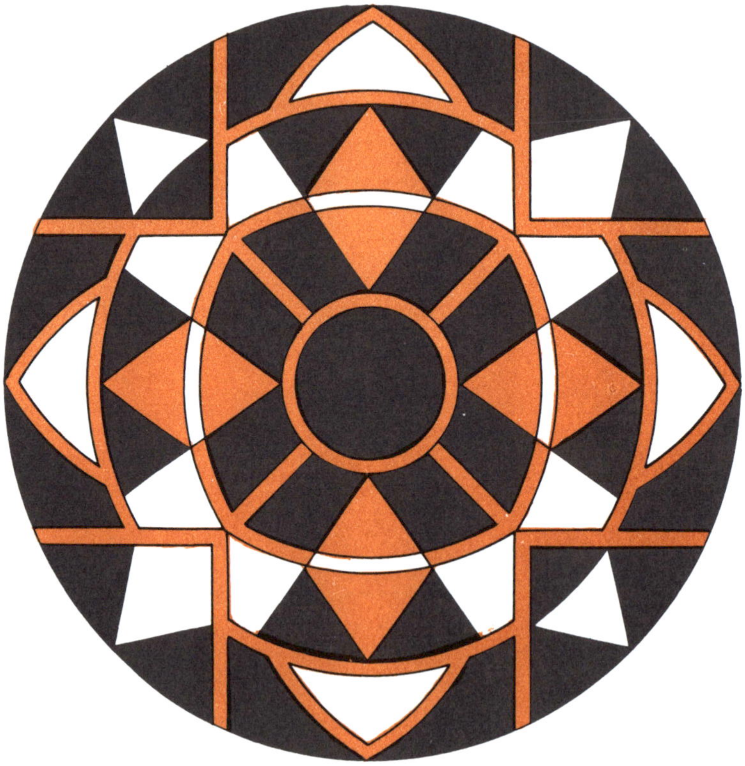

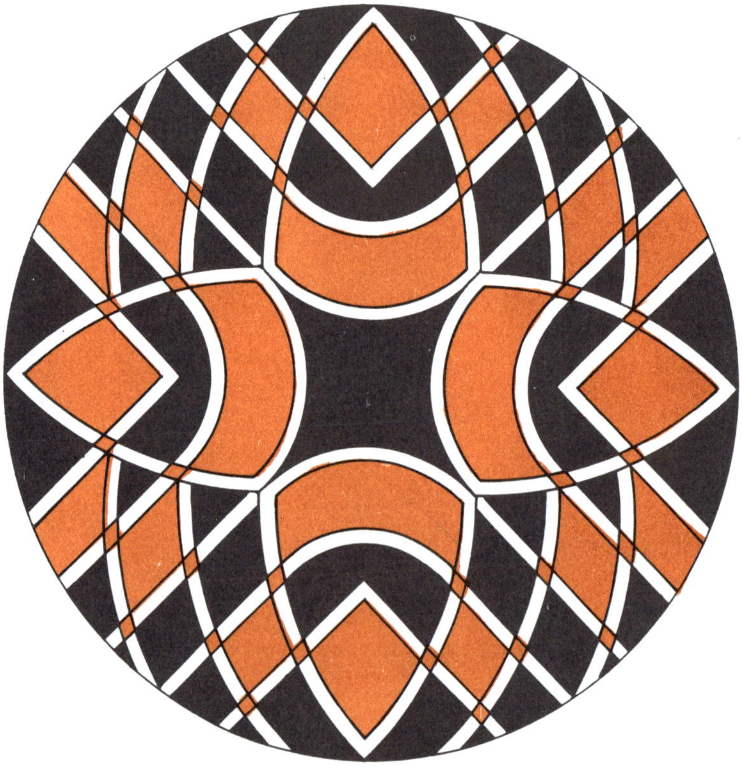

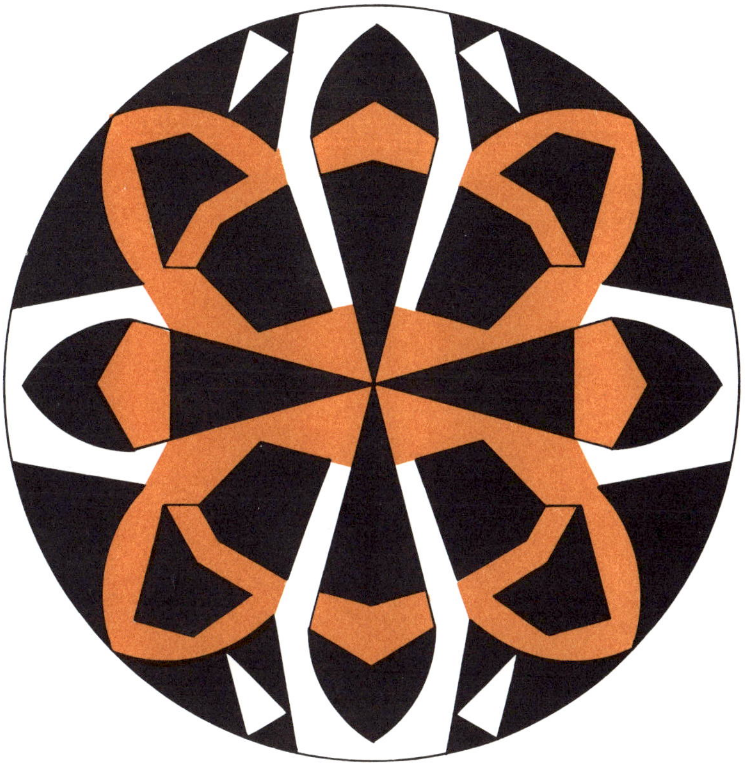

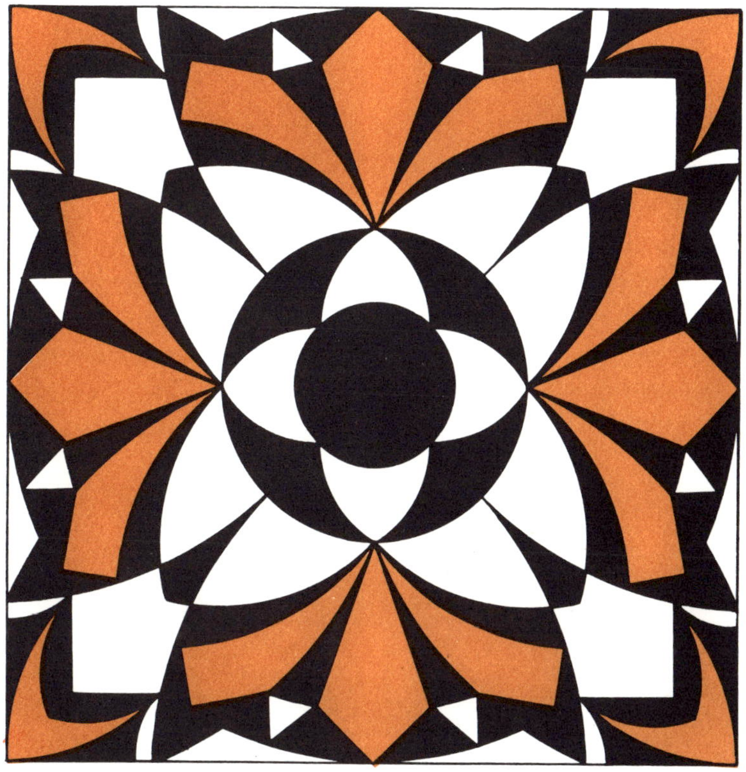

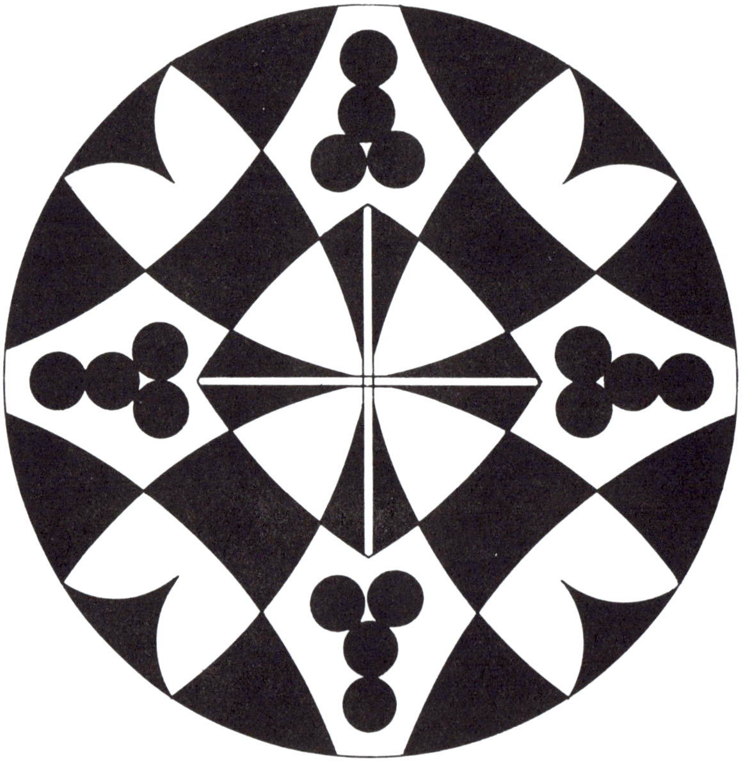

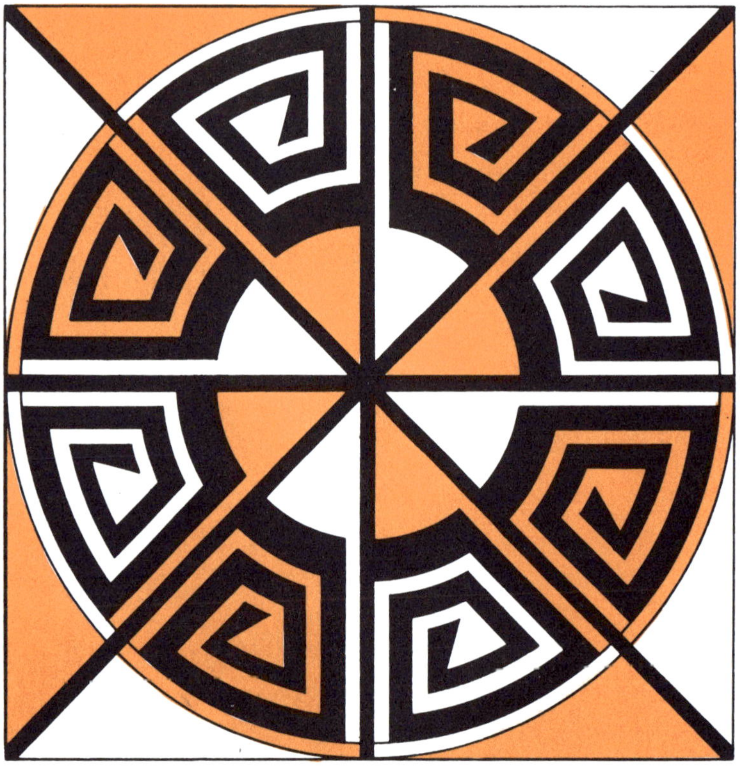

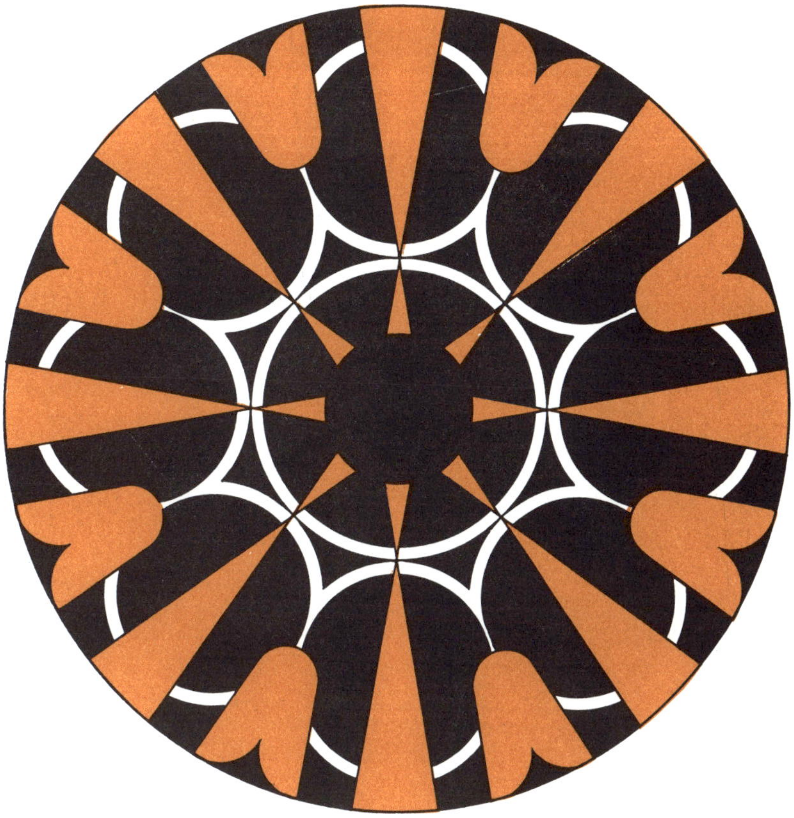

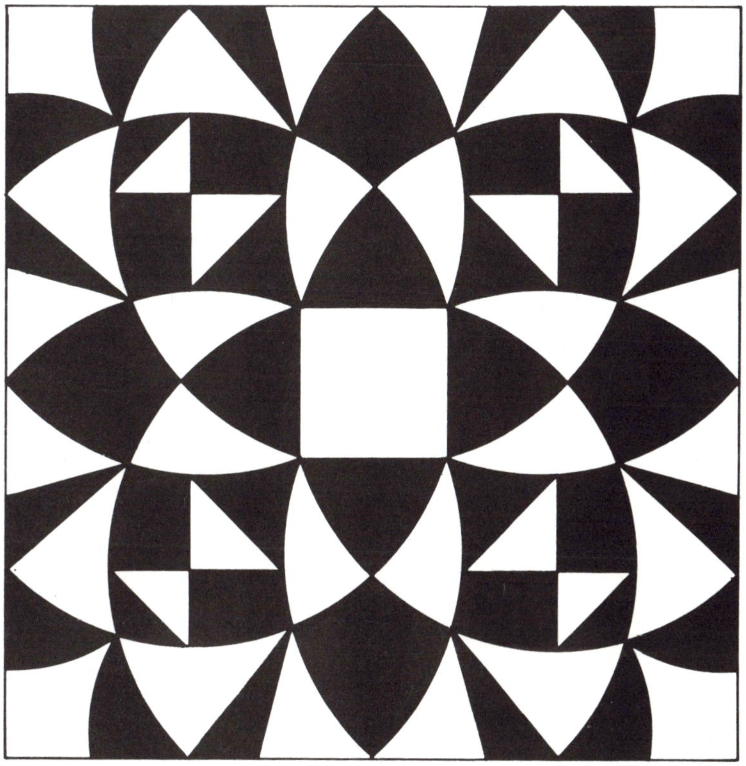

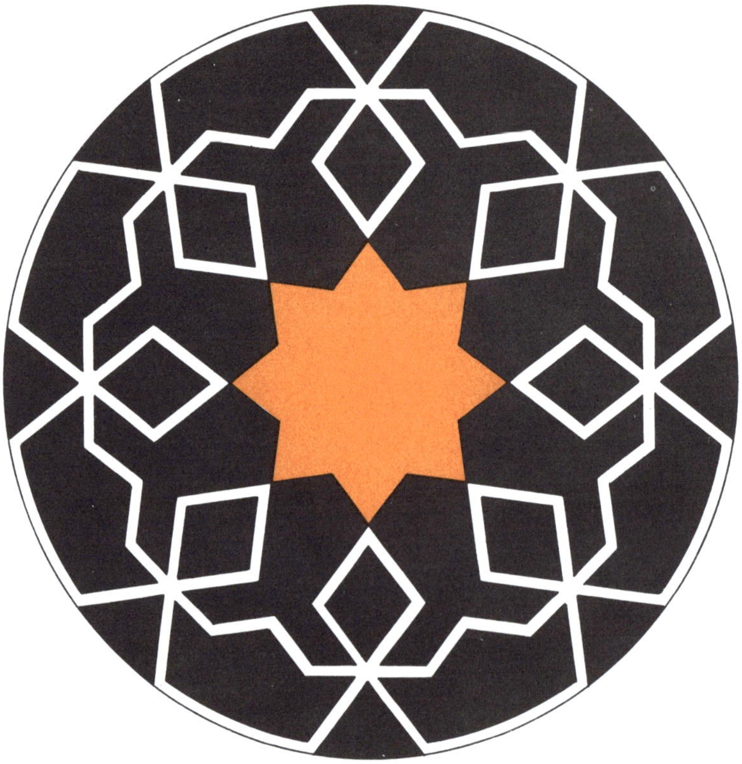

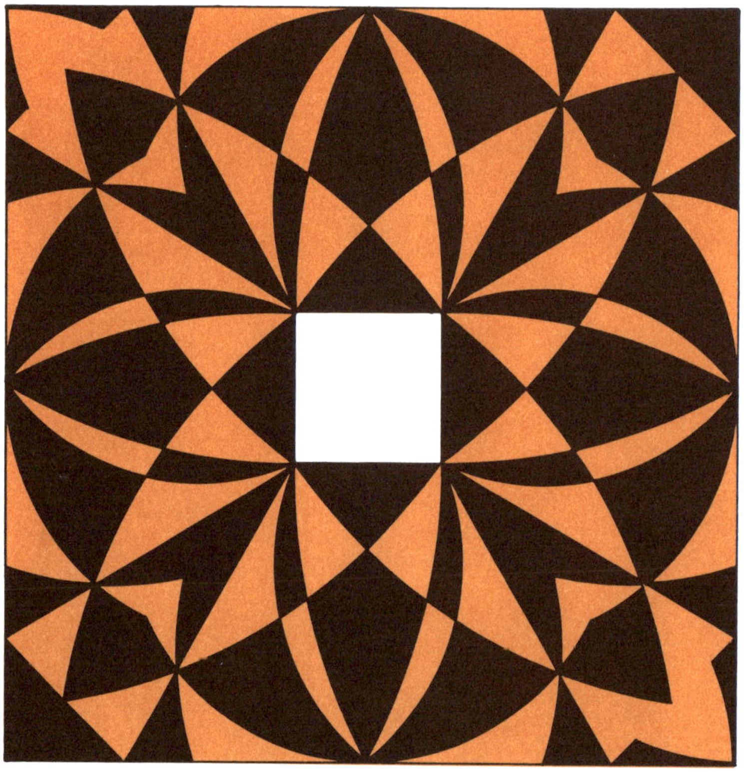

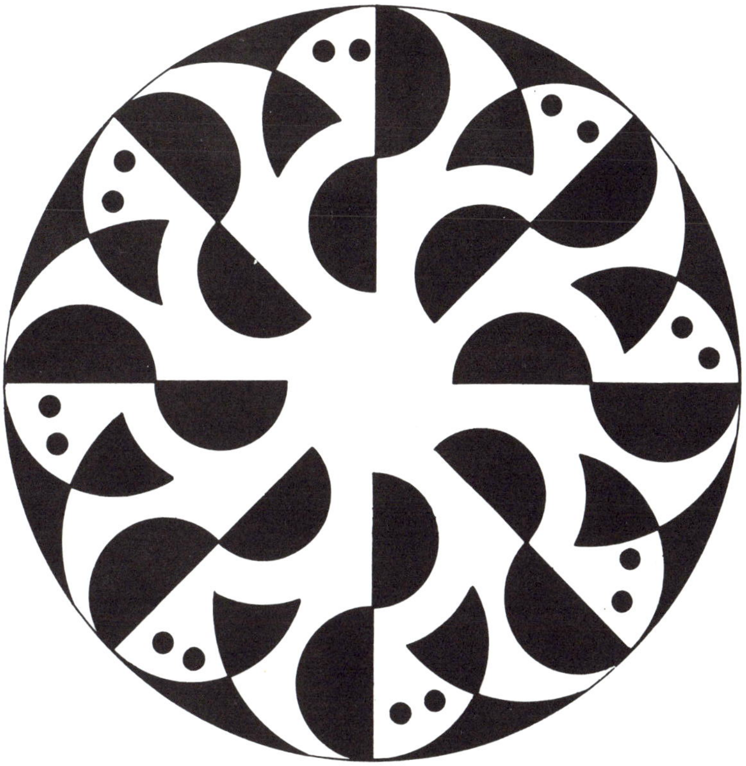

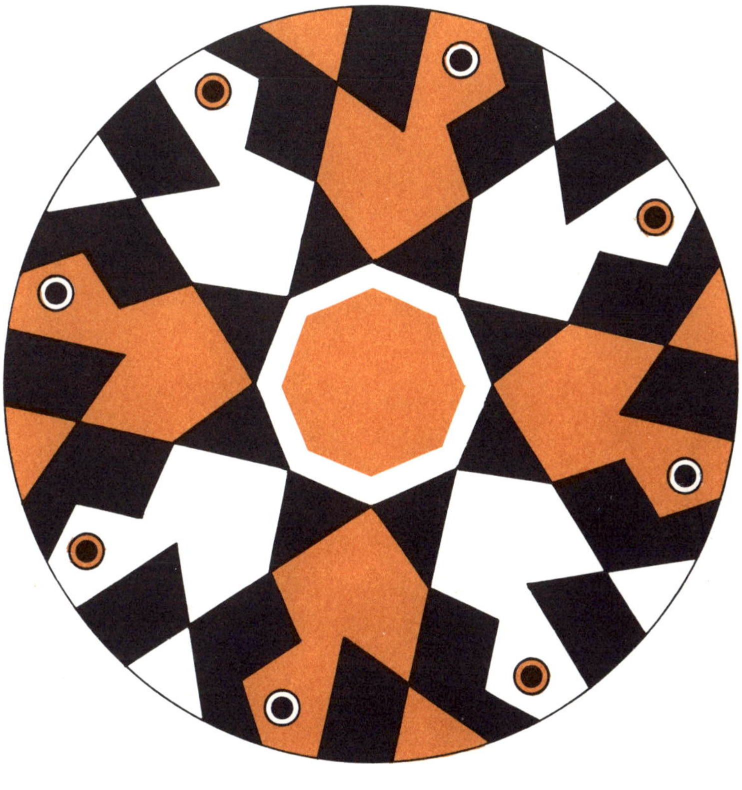

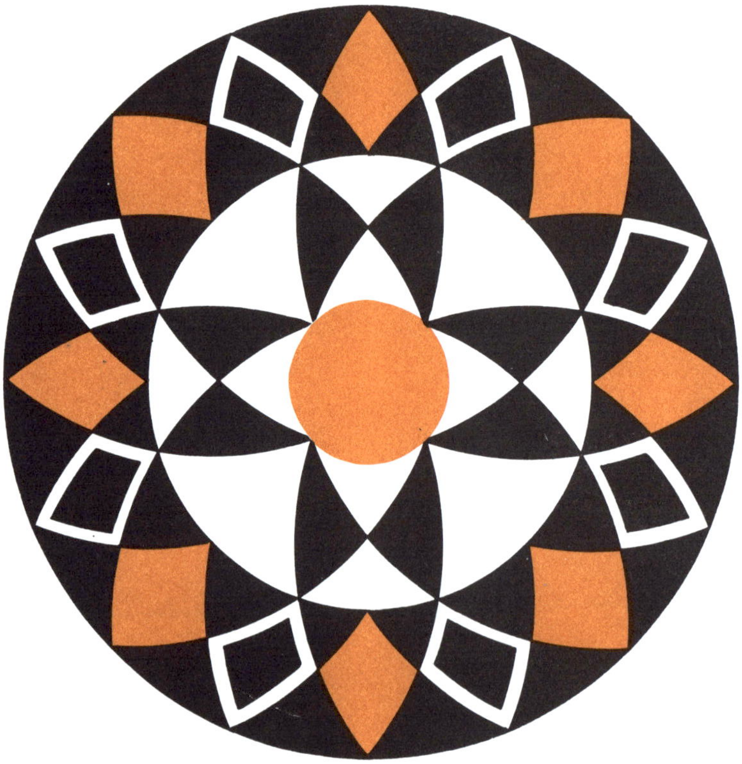

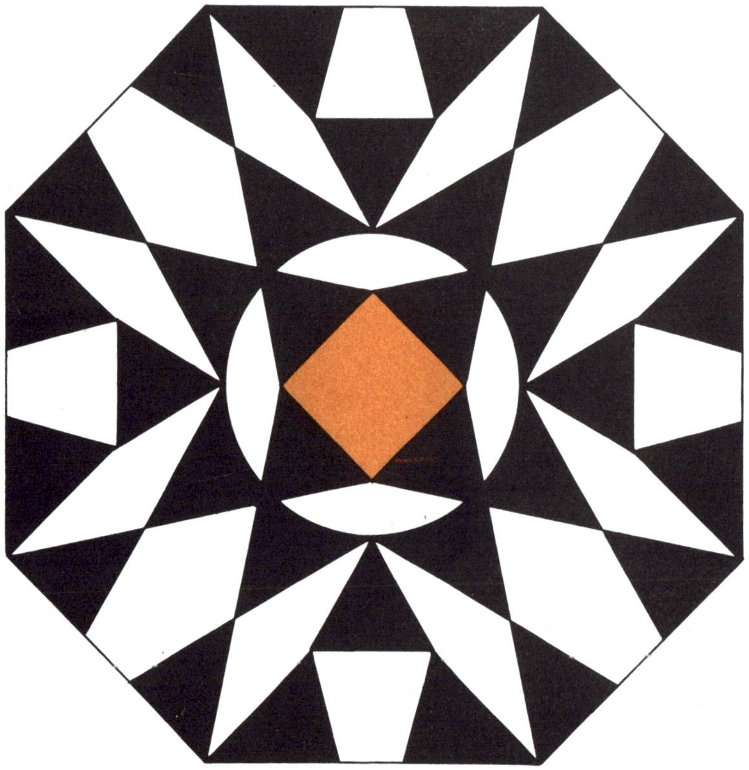

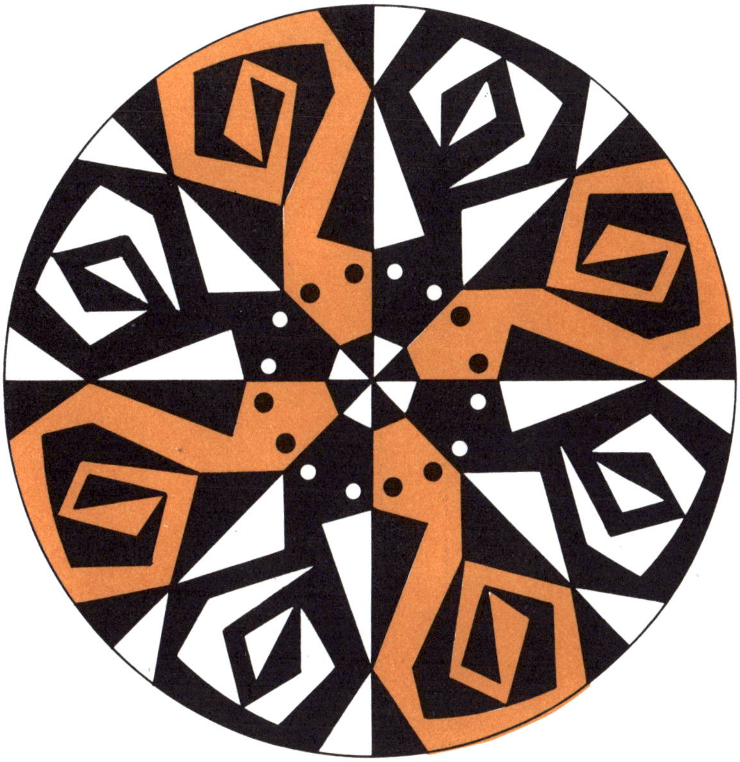

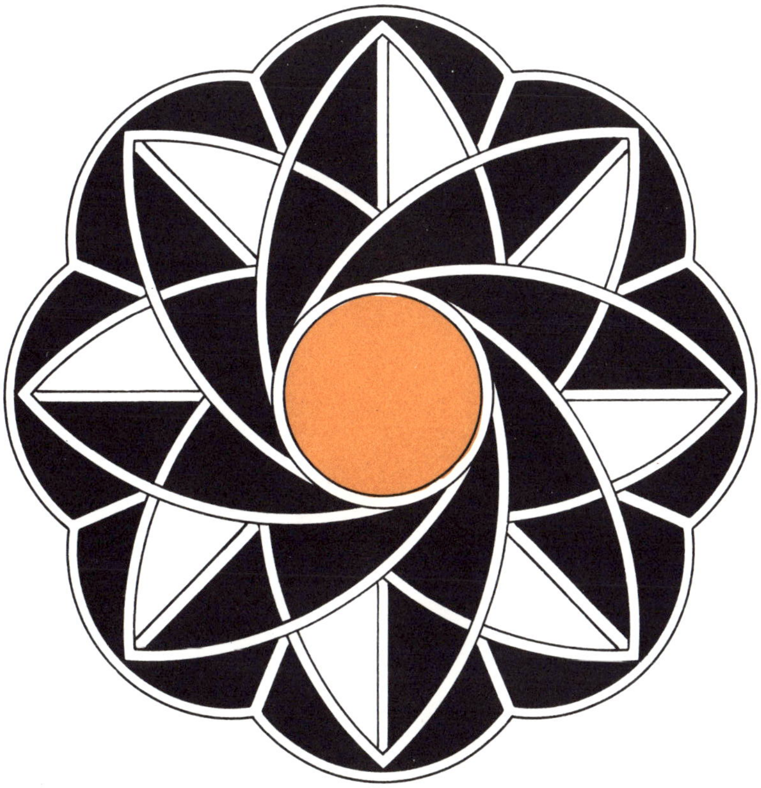

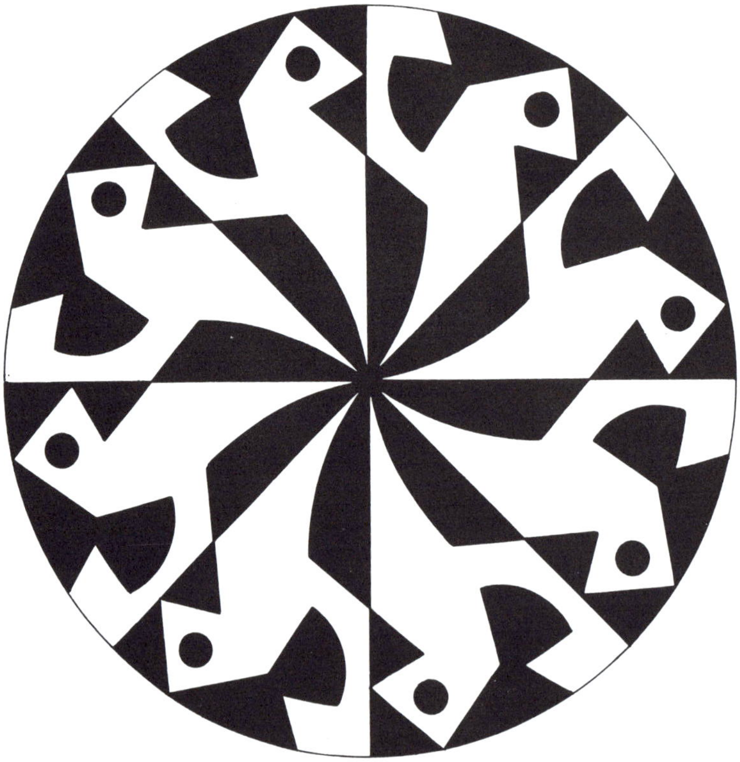

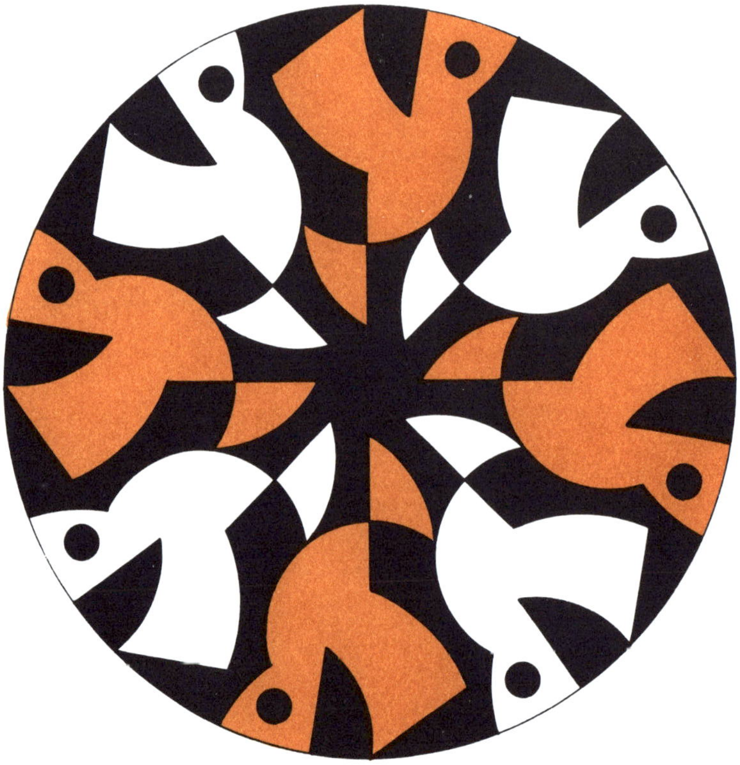

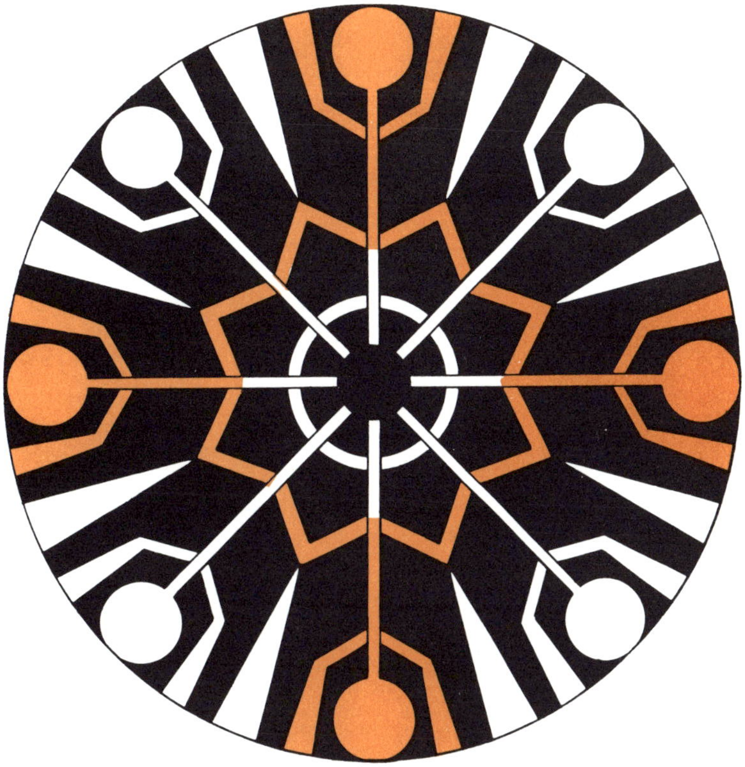

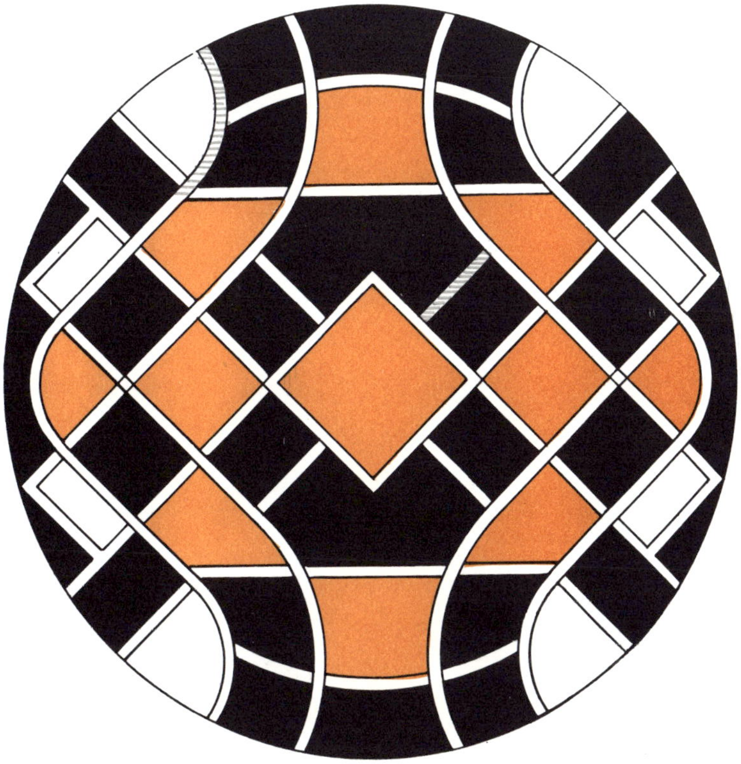

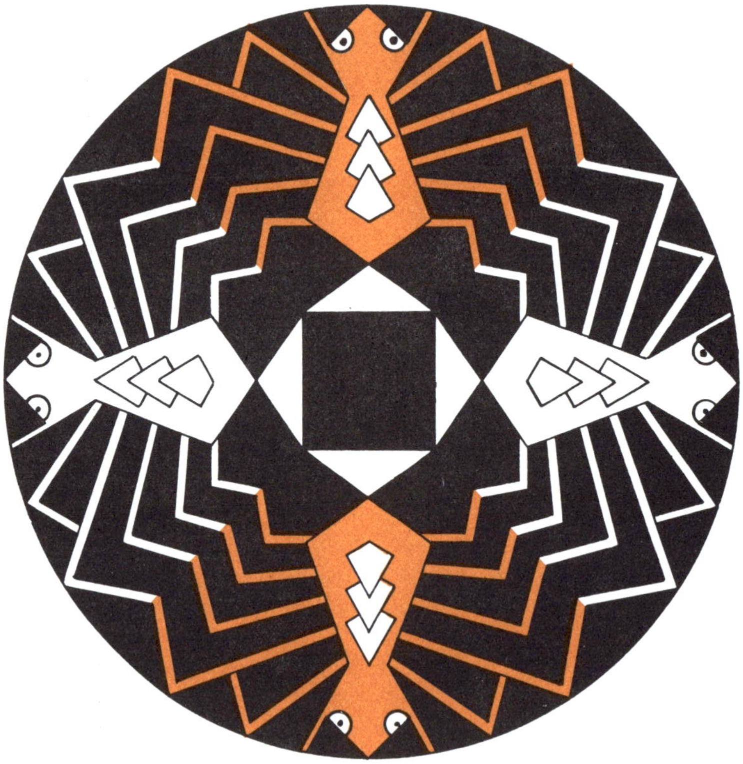

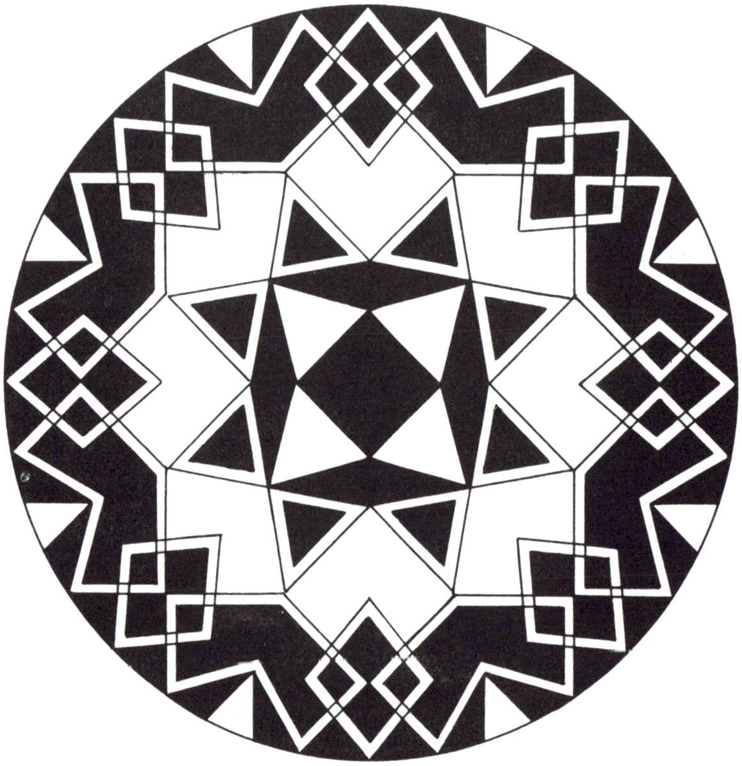

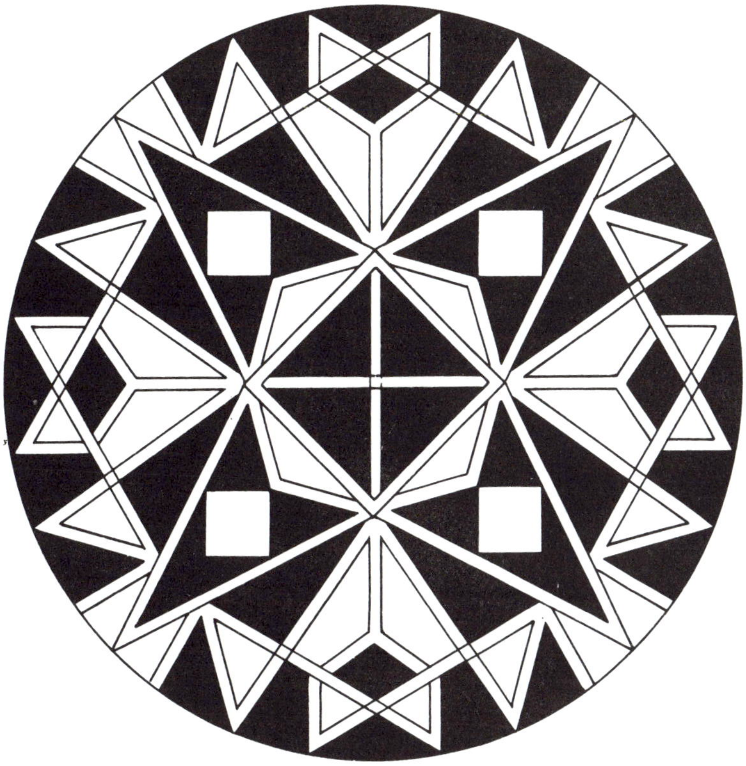

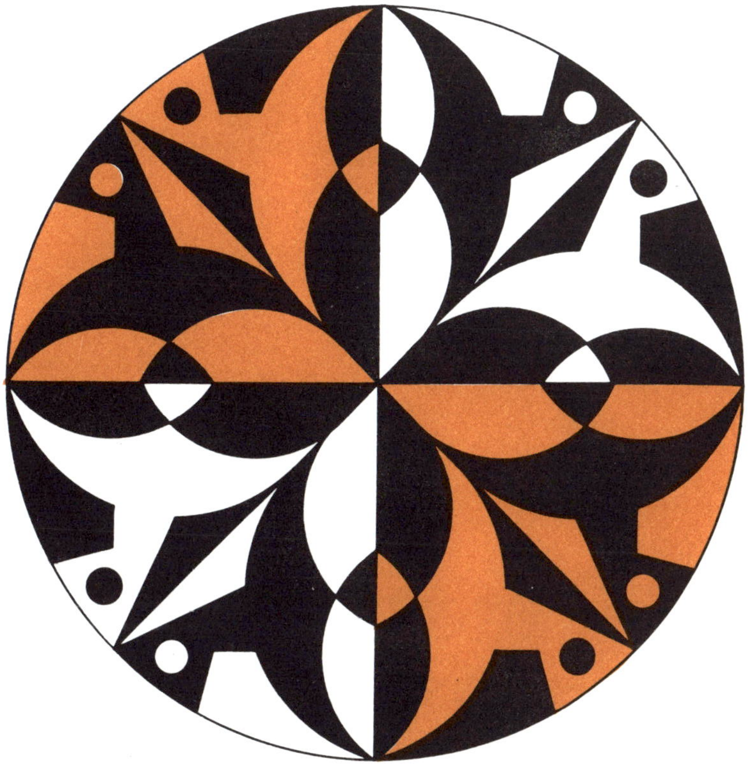

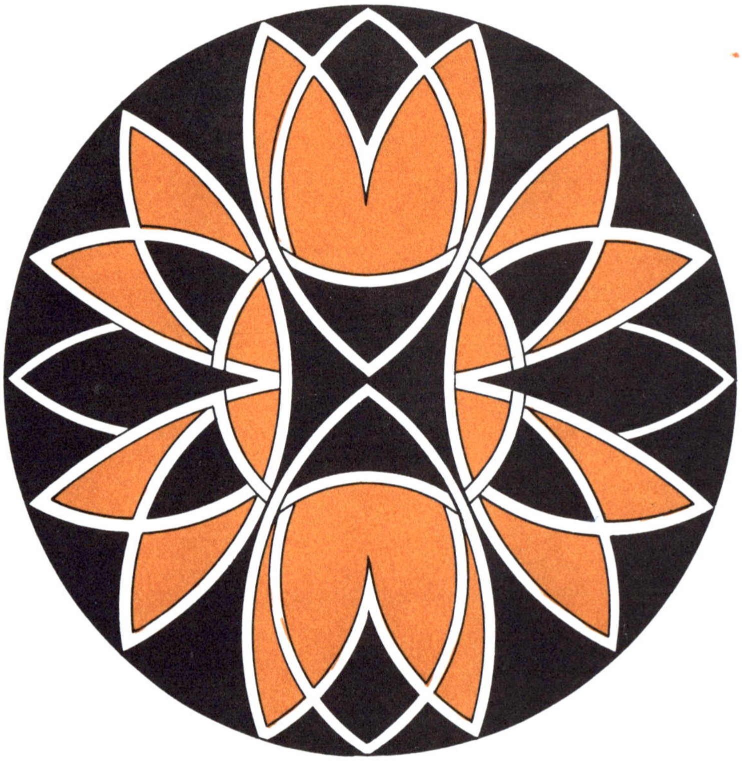

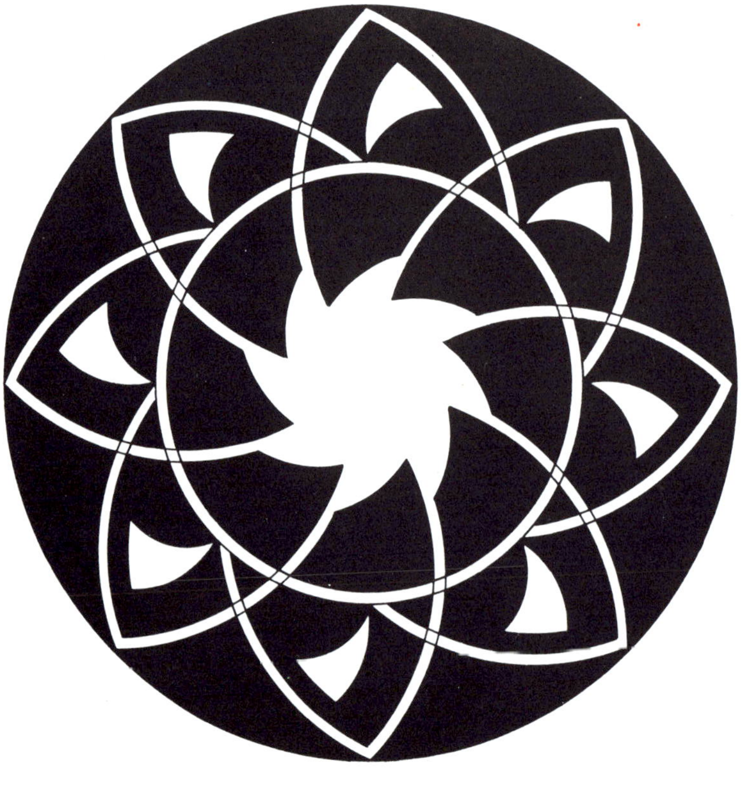

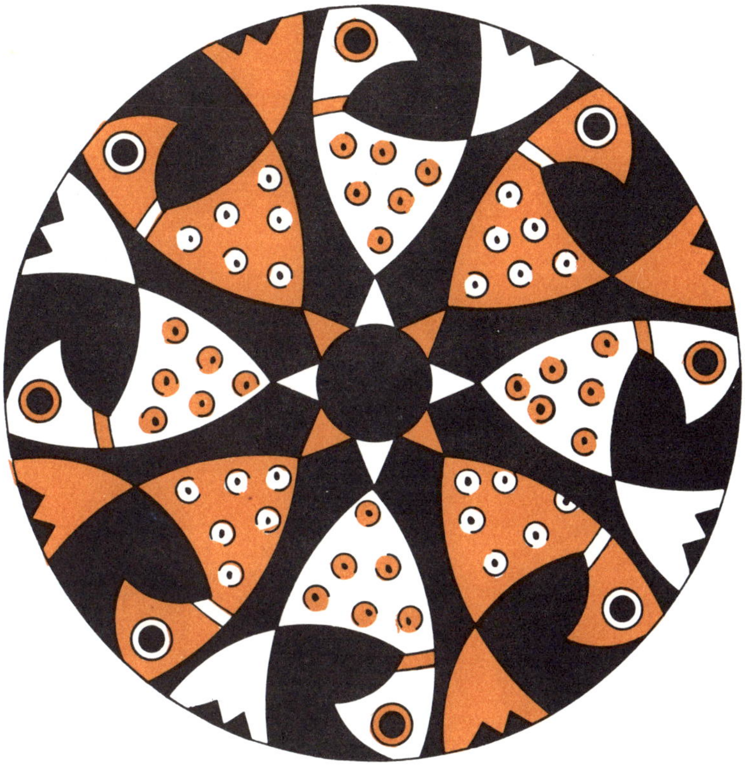

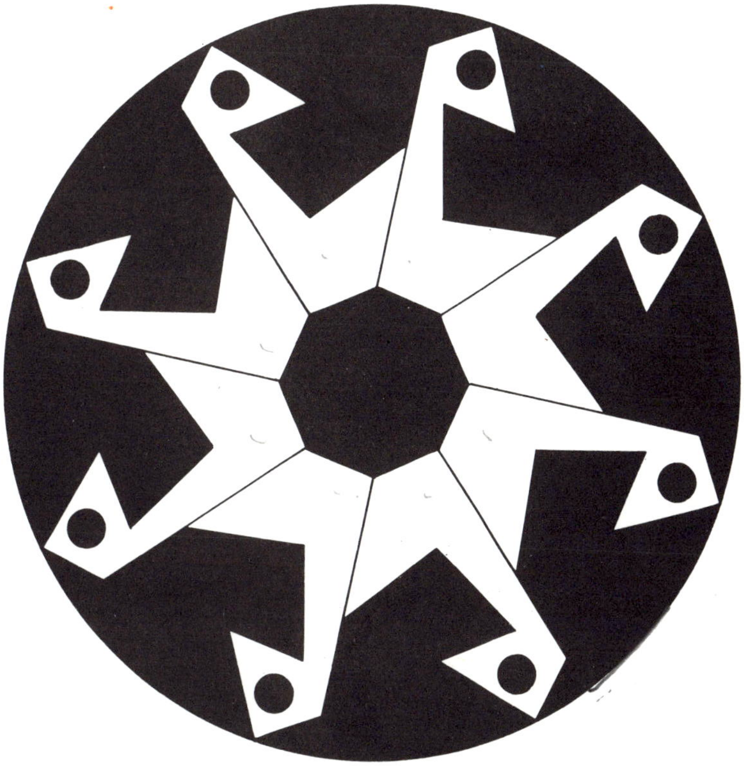

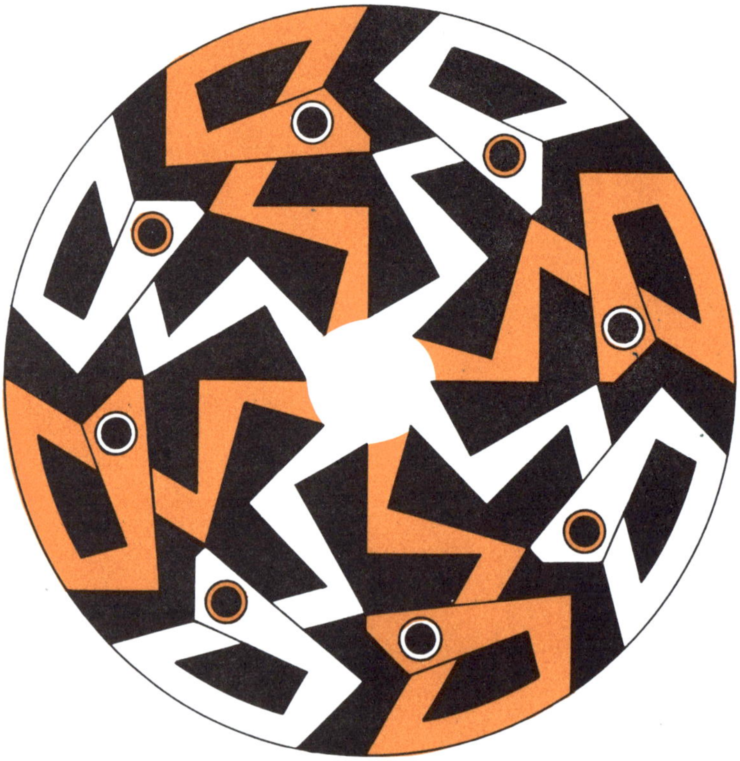

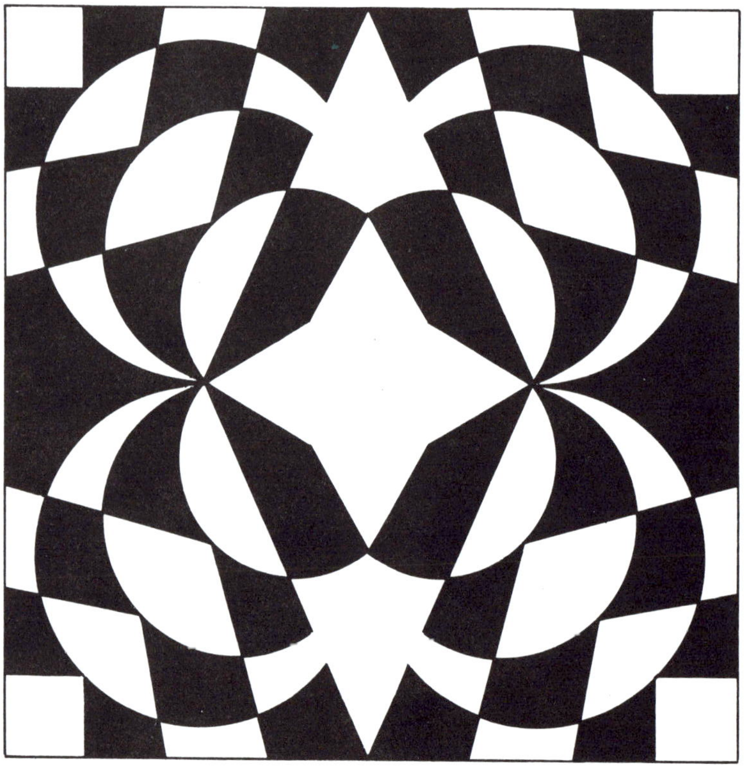